GCSE SCIENCE

COURSEWORK GUIDES

Stuart Farmer

Longman

EDITORS' PREFACE

The introduction of GCSE created many challenges for both teachers and pupils, not least the idea that, for most subjects, the grade awarded should be based not only on examination performance but also on the assessment of certain pieces of coursework. Whilst this concept has been welcomed in most educational circles as relieving some or all of the stress associated with examinations, it is also recognised as imposing other sorts of pressures on pupils. To achieve good results, it is necessary to keep up to date, be organised, and most importantly, maintain an appropriate standard *from the beginning of the course*.

Longman Coursework Guides have been written by experienced examiners to give GCSE candidates help with such tasks as choosing, researching and writing up topics. In addition, the authors give many examples of (and comments upon) typical student assignments.

We believe that the books will stimulate as well as instruct, and will enable students to produce coursework which will truly reflect the level of commitment and effort which the GCSE demands.

Geoff Black and Stuart Wall

LONGMAN COURSEWORK GUIDES

SERIES EDITORS
Geoff Black and Stuart Wall

TITLES AVAILABLE
Art and Design
Biology
Business Studies
CDT: Design and Realisation
Chemistry
Computer Studies
Economics
English
English Literature
Geography
Mathematics
Physics
Religious Studies
Science
Social and Economic History
World History

Longman Group UK Limited,
Longman House, Burnt Mill, Harlow,
Essex CM20 2JE, England
and Associated Companies throughout the world.

© Longman Group UK Limited 1989
All rights reserved; no part of this publication may be reproduced, stored in a retrieval system, or transmitted in any form or by any means, electronic, mechanical, photocopying, recording, or otherwise, without the prior written permission of the Publishers.

First published 1989

British Library Cataloguing in Publication Data

Farmer, Stuart
Science.
1. England. Secondary schools. Curriculum subjects: Science. G.C.S.E. examinations. Techniques
I. Title
507′.6

ISBN 0-582-05183-5

Produced by The Pen and Ink Book Company, Huntingdon, Cambridgeshire

Set in 10/11pt Century Old Style

Printed and bound in Great Britain by
William Clowes Limited, Beccles and London

CONTENTS

CHAPTER 1

THE NATURE AND IMPORTANCE OF COURSEWORK

UNIT 1 INTRODUCTION TO COURSEWORK

Wherever you study for your GCSE in Science you will have to do practical work. Some of this practical work will be **coursework**, which is assessed by your subject teacher during lessons. It counts, along with end-of-module tests or exams, towards your final GCSE grade. These tests of your practical skill usually account for *at least* 20% of your exam mark, and often more.

Most of your coursework will occur 'naturally' as part of the learning process in Science, not as special tests added on to your course for assessment purposes. For success in coursework it is vital that you consider **all** your coursework important, not just those pieces which are assessed. Coursework can make a very important contribution to your success in Science.

1.1 National requirements in Science

The different Science courses are based on agreed National standards, so that the grade from one Examination Group is of a similar standard to that from another. All syllabuses are written in a common style, each containing a list of the aims and assessment objectives, a scheme of assessment with percentage weightings, grade descriptions and, of course, the subject content (see Unit 4 of this chapter).

Many new syllabuses meet the requirements contained in the *National Criteria for the Sciences : Double Award* and will contain the same 'common core of content'. All current Science syllabuses will satisfy, at the very least, the *National Criteria for Science*. These various criteria are nationally agreed statements of the aims, objectives, content and assessment methods to be followed, and they exist for all the subjects examined in the GCSE.

UNIT 2 COURSEWORK IN SCIENCE SYLLABUSES

2.1 Types of Science syllabus

> **In co-ordinated and combined science courses, the separate subjects of Biology, Chemistry and Physics will still be obvious. This is not the case for integrated science courses.**

There are many types of Science course available, but yours will certainly be either **Co-ordinated, Combined** or **Integrated.** In 'co-ordinated' or 'combined' Science courses, the separate components of Biology, Chemistry and Physics will still be obvious. Here the separate sciences will support each other, overlapping at times in order to make the Science broad and balanced. However, in 'integrated' Science courses the components of Science are so well mixed that they may not be apparent at all.

If your course is **modular** then it might be either co-ordinated, combined or integrated. Modules are free-standing units of learning which may be grouped with other modules to form a complete course. Each module has its own specific aims and assessments. These fit together to give an overall pattern for the Science course. Not all your practical skills will be assessed in any one module. Nevertheless, by the end of your course each skill will have been assessed several times.

Whatever the Science course you are following, it will lead to either one (single) or two (double) GCSE grades, depending on how much time you spend studying Science at school or college.

Most Science syllabuses contain a description of the criteria or standards used for assessing practical skills during coursework and examinations. We summarise these standards for Double Award Science below, after giving an overview of the various Science courses available, and the importance of coursework in each one.

2.2 Coursework requirements in Science syllabuses

Fig 1.1 outlines the importance of coursework in the various GCSE Science courses.

Exam Group	Course	Percentage of total mark
LEAG	Science (Combined – Single/Double)	20%
LEAG	Science (Syllabus M – Single/Double)	25%
LEAG	Science (Syllabus N – Single/Double)	30%
LEAG	The Sciences – Double Award (Combined)★	20%
LEAG	The Sciences – Double Award (Modular)★	25%
LEAG	The Sciences – Double Award (Integrated)★	30%
MEG	Science (Syllabuses A & B – Single A/Double A+B)★	40% in A 25% Assignment in B
MEG	Science (Syllabus C – Single, limited to C max. grade)	25%
MEG	Science (Syllabus D – Double, limited to CC max. grade)	25%
MEG	Combined Science (Double)★	20%
MEG	Co-ordinated Science (Suffolk – Double)	45–60%
MEG	Nuffield Co-ordinated Science – Double★	30%
MEG	The Sciences (Hertfordshire – Double)★	30%
NEA	Science (Dual Award – Double, Integrated	Principles 50% Applications 25%
NEA	Science (Modular – Single/Double)	30%
NEA	The Sciences – Double Award (Modular)★	30%
SEG	Science (Single/Double)	20%
SEG	Integrated Science (Double)	25%
SEG	The Sciences – Double Award (Modular)	20%
SEG	The Sciences – Double Award (Co-ordinated)	25%
NISEC	Science (Single)★	30%
WJEC	Science (Single/Double)	20%
UCLES	IGCSE Combined Science (Single/Double)	20%

★ Denotes the new Balanced Science courses that meet the GCSE National Criteria for 'The Sciences: Double Award', at the time of writing.

Fig 1.1
Coursework in GCSE Science: practical/coursework marks

SKILLS AND ABILITIES IN DOUBLE AWARD SCIENCE

All GCSE Science courses involve the assessment of the same basic scientific skills. The most recent National Criteria are those for *The Sciences : Double Award.* Within these *Double Award* syllabuses, candidates are expected to demonstrate their experimental skills and abilities to:

“The vital experimental abilities and skills for Double Award Science.”

- Select or formulate propositions amenable to experimental test (see Chapter 3; Unit 3).
- Devise procedures and select apparatus and materials suitable for checking the validity of data, conclusions, generalisations, hypotheses and predictions (see Chapter 3; Units 2, 4 and 5).
- Follow instructions accurately for the conduct of experiments (see Chapter 2; Unit 2).
- Handle apparatus and materials effectively (see Chapter 2; Unit 3).
- Work with due regard for safety (Chapter 2; Unit 7).
- Observe, measure and record accurately and systematically (Chapter 2; Units 4 and 5).
- Carry out investigations (Chapter 3; Unit 1).
- Recognise and explain variability and unreliability in experimental measurements (see Chapter 2; Unit 6 and Chapter 3; Unit 5).
- Evaluate critically the design of experiments, experimental observations and other data and draw conclusions (see Chapter 2; Unit 6 and Chapter 3; Unit 5).

Don't worry about the wording in the descriptions above; it is not *your* problem to interpret these requirements, your teacher or lecturer will do that for you. Your aim must be to achieve high standards as a practical scientist, not only during assessment exercises, but throughout your course. This book is designed to help you achieve greater competence as a practical scientist, and as a result to gain credit for your practical skills in GCSE Science.

In Unit 4 of this chapter you will find summaries of the Practical Coursework Assessment details for some of the major GCSE Science syllabuses. Use these as a starting point for your own investigation of the syllabus you are actually working to. Every effort has been made to present the information as accurately as possible. However, you would be well advised to consult your teacher or to write to your Exam Group for the current syllabus. The addresses of the Exam Groups are given on page 15.

UNIT 3 HOW SCIENCE COURSEWORK IS ASSESSED

Most of the practical coursework that is assessed during your course will be organised by your teacher or lecturer. However, on occasions *you* will have considerable responsibility for the practical work, especially when your problem-solving skills are being tested. These skills are often assessed when you design and carry out experiments of your own.

The typical example of a practical coursework exercise given below is teacher-organised and only two skills have been selected for assessment. Usually such exercises form an important part of the work you are doing at the time and will be closely linked to recent lessons and to those that are to follow. Practical coursework is almost always part of your normal work in Science. It is not something special or out of place, so if you are unfamiliar with the example below, don't worry. Your teacher or lecturer would not expect you to carry out exercises before you have reached the appropriate stage in your course.

3.1 A typical coursework assessment

In this example on electrolysis the teacher chose to assess only the skills of *observation* and *design*, even though all of the following practical skills were involved. As you read through them, note that each skill is dealt with in much greater detail in the specified Units of Chapters 2 and 3.

PRACTICAL SKILLS

Following instructions

See Chapter 2; Unit 2. Your teacher or lecturer will probably introduce the lesson by explaining how the practical coursework exercise that is to be assessed fits into the work you are doing. If there are any new things to explain *before* you start, they will probably be discussed at this time, so listen carefully. Often a worksheet like the one in this example (Fig 1.2, page 4) will be provided. Read and look at it thoroughly before starting. If you feel that some help is needed, **now** is the time to ask. However, be patient – you may not be the only student wanting help. It would not be difficult to assess the skill of following instructions using this exercise.

Selecting and handling apparatus and materials

See Chapter 2; Unit 3. There would be ample opportunity for your teacher or lecturer to assess these skills, as there is a lot of work to be done before and after making observations.

Observing and measuring

See Chapter 2; Unit 4. The teacher who designed this exercise planned to assess the skill of *observation*, and so provided opportunity for this on the worksheet. It would have been possible to add some *measurement* tasks as well, such as measuring volumes of gases produced at the anode and cathode in a given time. Be sure to concentrate on the *actual tasks* given on the sheet; in this example there are clear hints about what observations are expected.

GCSE SCIENCE PRACTICAL ASSESSMENT

DATE ____________

OBSERVE /

DESIGN /

NAME ____________ STG ____________

This assessment is in two parts, done in any order.

PART ONE AIM: To investigate the electrolysis of salt solution.

APPARATUS: Clamp/stand, cell & test tube (as diagram), 2 wires, 2 croc clips, power supply. Access to flame, splints, indicator, 30ml salt solution in beaker.

METHOD:

(a) Wash the cell & electrodes thoroughly under running water. Set it up as shown.

(b) Almost fill the cell with salt solution.

(c) Add JUST enough indicator to be visible.

(d) Prepare a tube for gas collection by filling with solution, inverting without loss, mouth down in the cell (but not over any particular electrode YET).

(e) Pass dc electricity at 6V p.d. Something should be visible after a few seconds. If not, check circuit for faults or seek help.

(f) Observe as much as possible over a couple of minutes. Collect any gases and identify them if possible by tests (incl. lit/glowing splint).

DIAGRAM:

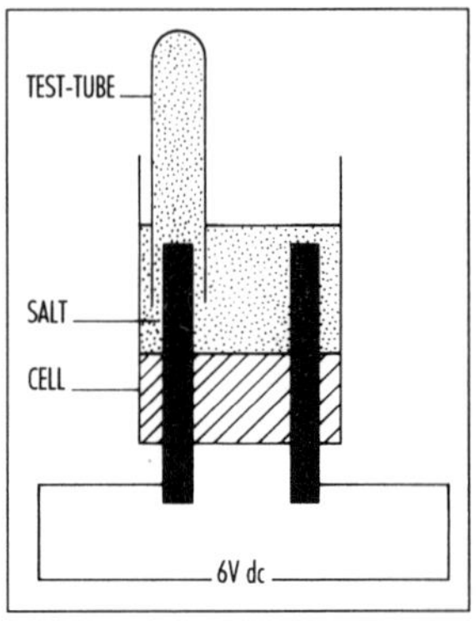

OBSERVATIONS

At Cathode: ____________

At Anode: ____________

In the Solution: ____________

PART TWO AIM: To deal with problems in electrolysis circuits.

"HANDS ON" TIME LIMIT: 10 minutes.

SITUATION

A pupil has set up three circuits to study the electrolysis of:

(A) Dilute sulphuric acid.

(B) Dilute hydrochloric acid.

(C) Magnesium sulphate solution.

Experiment (C) works well and the bulb lights to prove it (check this). However, the pupil has complained that "nothing is happening" in (A) or (B).

TASK NOTES

(i) IDENTIFY the faults or causes of failure.

(ii) You do not actually have to CORRECT the faults but you may carry out any test, including temporary alterations to the apparatus.

(iii) However, do not endanger the apparatus or yourself by over-loading or short circuiting and it is essential that you eventually leave the apparatus EXACTLY as you found it.

(iv) You may use only the apparatus supplied.

(v) There may be MORE THAN ONE problem, and they may be of ANY TYPE.

There may be more than one set of apparatus (with different errors). If this is the case, say which set you used .....

REPORT: Reasons for lack of results in ....

(A) ____________

(B) ____________

When finished with the apparatus, put EVERYTHING back as it was & call the teacher to check.

Fig 1.2
GCSE practical worksheet

Recording and communication

See Chapter 2; Unit 5. The observations made during the electrolysis of the salt solution should be *recorded* in the spaces provided on the worksheet, but care must be taken to plan your comments before writing them in. If possible, write them out in rough before finally completing the worksheet. All your observations must be clearly stated. There is little opportunity in this exercise to show that you can record data in a suitable form, such as a table of results.

Interpreting information

See Chapter 2; Unit 6. In the example of Fig 1.2 there is some *interpretation* necessary in the testing and identifying of any gases produced, and in the reporting of problems in electrolysis circuits. Any interpretations you make should be based on the data you have actually collected; it is the *use* of this information that will attract credit. This skill was not assessed by the teacher who designed the exercise and will therefore be fully dealt with on other more appropriate occasions.

Following safe working procedures

See Chapter 2; Unit 7. It is assumed that you, and other students, will always follow *safe working procedures*, even though you will only be assessed on this skill once or twice. There would be ample opportunity in this example to check your safe use of electrical equipment, conduct of gas testing, handling of acids and other chemicals, etc.

3.2 How assessment takes place

“Formative assessment lets you know how you are getting on.”

Your teacher or lecturer continually monitors your progress. This may be in your *practical work* in the laboratory, your *written work* done at home and in class, and your *oral contribution* during lessons. Often you will get *feedback* about your progress, or lack of it, in the form of a mark out of ten, a nod of approval, or specific written comments about errors in your work. Such appraisal and feedback are often called *formative assessment.* This type of assessment lets you know how you are getting on. Your coursework in GCSE Science should fit into this category. Besides providing performance data that will contribute to your final GCSE grade, coursework should enable you to gain a fuller understanding of your strengths and weaknesses so that you can be guided towards higher achievement in the future.

In Science, it is unlikely that *all* the students in a class will be assessed during the same lesson, unless the class is small or the skills being assessed do not need to be observed. Recording and communication skills, for instance, could be assessed for a whole class, because in this case written reports could be marked after the lesson.

“Most skills will be tested several times during the course.”

It is usual for *half* of a class to be assessed, while the other half do some alternative self-directed work that does not require the full attention of the teacher or lecturer. However when you work in small groups, sometimes one student will be singled out for assessment, along with other single members of other groups.

It is unlikely that you will be assessed on any more than two or three skills in a practical session, but you will almost certainly be assessed several times for any given skill throughout your course. So if you fail to demonstrate a particular skill to the best of your ability, you will usually be given further opportunities to show that you do have that skill. Skills are assessed *independently* of each other. So if you achieve full marks in one skill and low marks in another during a particular coursework exercise, the full marks will still be recorded for one of the skills.

The restriction in the number of students being assessed, and in the number of skills being assessed, makes assessment easier for the teacher or lecturer and fairer for you. Focusing on a few students and on a narrow range of skills means that there is time for the job to be done properly, giving all students the opportunity to demonstrate their best performance.

“You can always ask which skills are being assessed during the practical.”

Examining Groups have specified that students should be *aware* of the range of skills in which they will be assessed during the course. However it is not general practice to inform students *which* particular skills will be assessed during each assessment exercise. If you are *not* told which individual skills are to be assessed on a particular occasion, it will do no harm to ask politely for that information. The Examining Groups do not usually instruct teachers and lecturers to be secretive about your coursework assessment marks. However, individual teachers vary in their views about the disclosure of marks. Usually you will find it easy to find out your mark for *individual exercises,* though not your final *total* mark for the coursework component of GCSE Science. There is often a good reason for this, since the final total may be arrived at in a rather complicated way.

There is, of course, some danger in knowing what your marks are! You may become discouraged if they are consistently low, or complacent if they are consistently high. Some schools and colleges will have their own policies about the availability of such knowledge, as will some teachers. However current practice seems to favour openness and sharing.

Thorough and detailed records of your coursework are very important. The Examination Groups usually request each *centre* (e.g. a school or college) to forward their marks in March or April, well before you take the final written examination. The written parts of your coursework assessment will probably be stored for you by your teacher or lecturer in a *coursework file.* Each candidate will have one of these and it is important that they are not lost. Examination Groups often use coursework files to check standards between different centres, and the consistency of marking within each centre. This process, called *moderation,* is important if the GCSE grades awarded are to be fair to all the candidates on a particular Science course.

The marks for each candidate are kept on an individual *record card,* which will look something like the example in Fig 1.3. Though the design of these will vary considerably, all will contain every coursework mark obtained by an individual. In preparing your final mark, only your *best* performances for each skill will be chosen by your teachers and examiners. These best scores will probably be entered onto a special summary sheet for all the Science GCSE candidates registered at your centre.

GCSE COURSEWORK PRACTICAL RECORD

SCIENCE

NAME: TRACEY JONES STG: FRB PTG: XIP 26

DATE	INIT	1	2a	2b	2c	3a	3b	4a	4b	5a	5b	EXPERIMENT	No
		4	1	1	2	2	2	3	1	2	2	Maximum marks	
SEPT. 87	DR.	3										MICROSCOPY	1
OCT. 87	CJM.					2	1			2	2	CO_2 TESTING	2
													3
													4
													5

FINAL GRADES:

Skill	1	2	3	4	5	TOTAL/40	%
Mark 1							
Mark 2							

KEY: 1 Follow instructions
2 Technique:
a) Selection b) Use c) Safety
3 a) Observation b) Measurement
4 Problem solving:
a) Design b) Application
5 a) Conclusion b) Calculations

Fig 1.3
Individual record card

3.3 Organisation of an assessment session

Internal practical assessment (rather than a practical exam set by an Examination Group) makes every teacher or lecturer into an examiner for their students. Although this may bring a new tension to teacher-student relationships, and an extra workload for them both, there is much to be gained from the process. Coursework is organised by teachers. They exercise their professional skill and judgement to provide coursework which meets the needs of all abilities and all existing skill levels. The availability of laboratories and equipment may determine whether you work as an individual or in a group.

Practical assessment exercises fall into several basic formats:

CLASS ASSESSMENT

Here all students carry out a practical exercise designed to allow the assessment of one or two skills. Often half the group will do the practical while the other half work independently. By halving the number of students in this way the teacher can make time to record individual performances in skills that must be observed, such as *safe working practice* (see Chapter 2; Unit 7) or *handling apparatus* (see Chapter 2; Unit 3). In the next teaching session the situation would be reversed, with the other half doing the practical. This approach sometimes helps the teacher to cope with a student's planned, or unplanned, absence.

Half the class do practical round the edge of the laboratory and the others do theory in the middle.

Small group work

SELECTED ASSESSMENT

Here the whole class will be working, either individually or in groups. But only certain identified individuals will receive the focus of the teacher's attention for assessment purposes.

CIRCUS ASSESSMENT

Here the whole class carries out a series of short, practical exercises, arranged at *stations* around the laboratory. Often the teacher will only assess you by observation at one or two of the stations. Assessment at other stations might be based on your written record, or no assessment might be made at these other stations. Observing and measuring (see Chapter 2; Unit 4) could easily be assessed in this way.

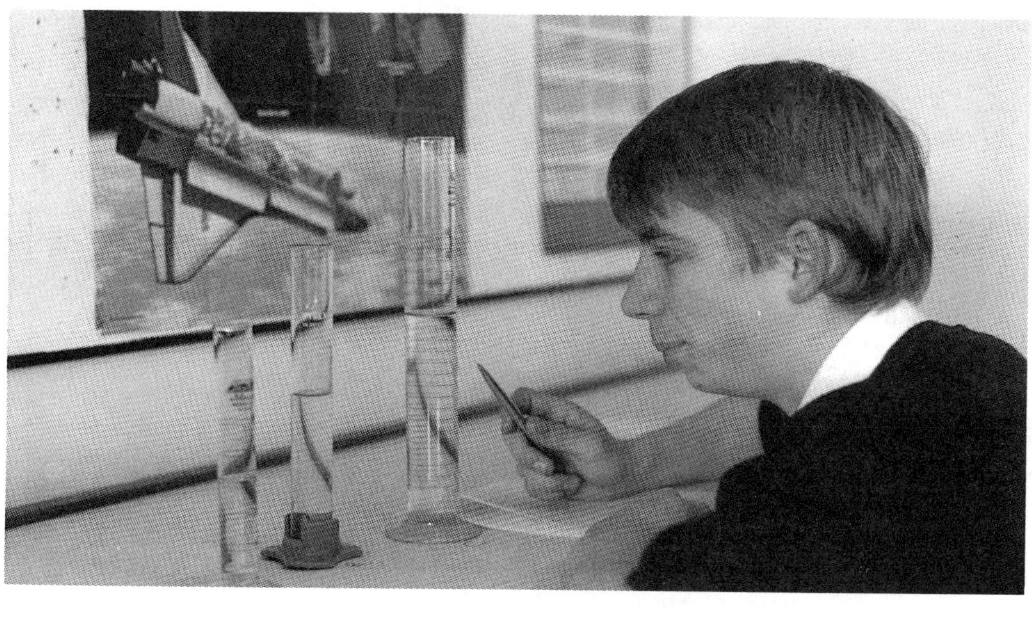

Station in a 'circus' practical session

OPEN-ENDED ASSESSMENT

Here students organise and carry out their practical activity to the best of their ability, either individually or in groups. This often involves *student-organised* investigations. This problem-solving approach usually involves all the skill areas we have identified so far.

ABILITY-RELATED ASSESSMENT

Here you may be asked to carry out a practical exercise that matches your ability, but one which might be different to the exercises that other students are doing in your class. Examination Groups ask teachers to avoid giving students tasks that are likely to result in them scoring zero; the exercises you are given should always allow you to show some 'positive achievement'. GCSE is about what you can do, not about what you can't! Some skills, such as *following instructions* (see Chapter 2; Unit 2), should provide most students with high scores; while others, such as *interpreting information* (see Chapter 2; Unit 6), will ensure a variety of performance levels in any class.

However the practical session is organised, it is likely that your teacher or lecturer will be moving around the laboratory, making notes on a record sheet. To make the awarding of marks fair, they will not usually be awarded by 'impression marking', that is, when the teacher thinks: 'that looks like a 9 out of 10'. Instead a carefully planned check list will usually have been produced. Other teachers in your school or college should then give similar marks for a given performance if they use the same standard checklist. A partly completed example may be found in Fig 1.4. This is for an investigation into power (Watts), using a simple circuit consisting of a lamp, a variable power supply, an ammeter and a voltmeter. Some of the items on the list must be assessed *during* the practical session, while others can be assessed later, using the written report. In this case a maximum of ten marks can be obtained in total, though these relate to a variety of individual skills.

Fig 1.4
Teacher's record sheet

SCIENCE PRACTICAL ASSESSMENT **RECORD SHEET**

TOPIC – CURRENT ELECTRICITY SET = 25, TEACHER = FMR

DURING PRACTICAL	Mark possible / Name	Rachel Allot	Naomi Best	Loise Carney	Samantha Chappel	Neil Davey							
Serious attempt to assemble circuit. OR	1			✓									
Completion without major assistance, but does get meters correct way round. OR	2				✓								
Assembly with no assistance. Can include changes from previous design.	3	✓	✓			✓							
Some reading, possibly with help, OR	1			✓									
Five readings of current and voltage over range 0–6V.	2	✓	✓		✓	✓							
Interpolation or every reading with correct level of precision (2 decimal places).	1	✓	0	✓	✓	0							
Tabulated readings.	1	✓	0	✓	✓	✓							
AFTER PRACTICAL	TOTAL	10	8	7	9	6							
A correct column of power calculations.	1	✓	✓	✓	✓	0							
A valid graph.	1	✓	✓	✓	✓	0							
A conclusion of the form that power increases with increasing current.	1	✓	✓	✓	✓	0							
Score of 10 marks maximum													

Mark possible Name

3.4 Difficulties with coursework

There are all sorts of reasons why the coursework component of your GCSE can cause problems. However Examination Groups are well aware of them and you should discuss any special problems you have with your teacher or lecturer. Moving schools and absence through illness are two common problems, but these difficulties are often easily overcome. Physical handicaps too can often be overcome by arranging suitably personalised assessment tasks. If you have a problem, share it, and remember, GCSE is all about what you *can* do, not what you can't!

UNIT 4 EXAM GROUP REQUIREMENTS

These summaries of the practical/coursework assessment details for some of the science courses listed in Figure 1.1 will provide a quick reference for you before you obtain your *own* syllabus. They will give an indication of the similarity of requirements between the various courses and a reminder of the important details for your own course whenever you need it!

4.1 LEAG

SCIENCE (COMBINED – SINGLE/DOUBLE)

20% Coursework in both versions. 5 skills and abilities have been identified:

A Planning and organisation.
B Practical procedures and manipulative skills.
C Observation and measurement.
D Report writing and recording.
E Drawing conclusions and interpreting

For the *Double Science Award* – assess each three times on the basis of at least *six* experiments/exercises/investigations, including two problem-solving exercises and some work in each of the subject areas studied.
For the *Single Science Award* – assess each twice on the basis of at least *three* experiments/exercises/investigations, including one problem-solving exercise.
Moderation – Sample of work will be moderated by the Exam Group.

SCIENCE (SYLLABUS M – SINGLE/DOUBLE)

25% Coursework in both versions. 5 skills and abilities have been identified:

A Planning and organisation.
B Practical procedures and manipulative skills.
C Observation and measurement.
D Report writing and recording.
E Interpreting results and drawing conclusions.

Marks – 0 to 5 (six point scale)
For the *Single Science Award* – assess all at least *twice*.
For the *Double Science Award* – assess all at least *three* times.
Moderation – Samples of practical work will be moderated by the Exam Group.

SCIENCE (SYLLABUS N – SINGLE/DOUBLE)

30% Coursework in both versions. 5 skills and abilities have been identified:

A Planning and organisation.
B Practical procedures and manipulative skills.
C Observation and measurement.
D Report writing and recording.
E Interpreting results and drawing conclusions.

Marks – 0 to 5 (six point scale)

For the *Double Science Award*:

Section A: each of the above to be assessed *twice* on the basis of at least 4 experiments/exercises/investigations, including at least one problem-solving exercise.
Section B: each of the above to be assessed within Section B in *two* problem-solving exercises. Each exercise should be equivalent to two double lessons (total 2.5 hours) of practical work.

For the *Single Science Award,* section A only is studied, each ability assessed twice on the basis of 4 experiments/exercises/investigations, at least one of these should adopt a problem-solving approach.
Moderation – sample of practical assessments will be moderated by the Exam Group. Additional samples may be requested if necessary.

4.2 MEG

SCIENCE (SYLLABUSES A & B – SINGLE A/DOUBLE A + B)

40% in A; 25% Assignment in B.
4 experimental skills have been identified which apply to both coursework and assignment. Each skill operates on a six point scale.
Single Science Award is – Syllabus A only; *Double Science Award* is – Syllabus A & Syllabus B.

A Using and organising techniques, apparatus and materials.
B Observing, measuring and recording.
C Handling experimental observations.
D Planning, carrying out and evaluating investigations.

Submit the best two marks for coursework for syllabus A.
Apply each criterion (skills A–D) to assignment for syllabus B to generate a mark out of 24.
Assignment – this can take the form of extension work, or a new scientific concept (idea), fieldwork etc. It is intended that the assignment occupies about 15 hours of 'lesson' time with associated homework.
Moderation – internal moderation arrangement must be made to assess the students in each centre (school or college) to a common standard. External moderation will be conducted by post. Evidence of tasks set and how the marks are awarded for skills A–D is required. In addition, for skills B, C and D specified samples of written work are required. Some of the assignments will also be requested.

SCIENCE (SYLLABUS C – SINGLE); (SYLLABUS D – DOUBLE)

Syllabus C – Single; 25% Coursework, limited to maximum C grade.
Syllabus D – Double; 25% limited to maximum C Coursework grade.
Both these syllabuses have the same assessment based on these skills;

A Using and organising techniques, apparatus and materials.
B Observing, measuring and recording.
C Handling experimental observations and data.
D Planning, carrying out and evaluating investigations.

The best two marks for each skill are submitted to the Examination Group. It is expected that both the teaching and assessment of practical skills will take place throughout the course.

COMBINED SCIENCE (DOUBLE)

20% Coursework. 4 experimental skills have been identified:

A Using and organising techniques, apparatus and materials.
B Observing, measuring and recording.
C Handling experimental observations and data.
D Planning, carrying out and evaluating investigations.

Double Science Award – two best marks for each skill submitted on a six point scale for each skill.
Moderation – arrangements must be made in each examination centre to assess practical work to a common standard. External moderation will be conducted by post on samples of work from each centre.

CO-ORDINATED SCIENCE (SUFFOLK–DOUBLE)

45–60% Coursework. This is not so easy to explain for this course, and so the whole pattern of assessment is summarised.
There are **eight** skills and abilities assessed during this course. There is no final exam:

1a) Knowing
1b) Understanding
1c) Using knowledge
2 Using apparatus and measuring instruments
3 Observing
4 Planning and designing
5a) Communicating : spoken
5b) Communicating : non-spoken
6a) Exploring and investigating : practically
6b) Exploring and investigating : data search
7 Collaborating effectively (working with others)
8 Being aware of the application of scientific knowledge within the community.

Three forms of assessment are used for each module:

1 End-of-module tests (skills and abilities 1a), 1b) and 1c)). One per module. Teacher and student identify appropriate level (from 3 levels) of the test.
2 Can-do-tests (skill and ability 2). One or two of these are specified per module.
3 Criterion-matching (skills and abilities 3 - 8). Two specified per module.

For each of the skills and abilities there is a set of level statements for three levels, Foundation, Merit and Special.
Levels are achieved by matching evidence of performance to statements.

Weightings: Can-do-tests 10%; End-of-module tests 40–45%; Processes and skills 45–50%.

Moderation – this is carried out by schools and colleges which form local 'cluster groups' under the supervision of Area and Regional Moderators. Each teacher must attend one half-day cluster meeting a year. Generally, two teachers from each school attend each meeting. Before the meeting, each of these two teachers prepares a case study, one of which is presented at the meeting. Three marked tests from a recent module are also taken to the meeting for discussion.

NUFFIELD CO-ORDINATED SCIENCE–DOUBLE

Coursework is 30%. This course has been specifically designed to give as much emphasis to the processes and skills of science as it does to the knowledge and understanding of scientific ideas.
4 experimental and 2 non-practical skills have been identified:

A Using and organising techniques, apparatus and materials.
B Observing, measuring and recording.
C Handling experimental observations and data.
D Planning, carrying out and evaluating investigations.
E Communication.
F Working with others.

Centres are required to submit the best two marks for skills A to D inclusive and a single mark for skills E and F.
Moderation – internal moderation arrangements must be made to assess students in each centre to a common standard. Samples of written work will be requested for external moderation by the Examination Group.

THE SCIENCES (HERTFORDSHIRE – DOUBLE)

30% Coursework is required by this syllabus based on the Nuffield 13-16 scheme published by Longmans. Six skills have been identified:

A Observation
B Use of apparatus
C Investigation
D Communication
E Pattern finding
F Working with peers (other students, not Lords of the realm!).

Each of the skills A–E inclusive are to be assessed three times each, but F has only to be assessed once.

Moderation – arrangements must be made in each centre for the internal moderation of work. Written work and records relating to assessed work will be requested by the Examination Group for Moderation purposes.

4.3 NEA

SCIENCE (DUAL AWARD – DOUBLE, INTEGRATED)

Principles account for 50% and applications for 25% of the Coursework. 7 skills and abilities are identified in this syllabus:

Principles
1 Devising and planning experiments.
2 Performing experiments.
3 Interpreting data and finding patterns.
4 Reporting experimental work.

Applications
5 Devising and evaluating solutions to real life problems using science knowledge.
6 Assessing evidence and evaluating arguments.
7 Formulating and organising ideas to communicate with other people.

The final mark from 0-10 is submitted to the Examination Group and weighted accordingly.
Moderation – standardisation meetings will be used to establish the appropriate standards of performance for teachers to apply to the internally assessed skills. One teacher from each school is required to attend. A moderator from the Examination Group will normally visit each centre to carry out moderation of sample work from 10 candidates.

SCIENCE (MODULAR – SINGLE/DOUBLE)

30% Coursework with *six* skills and abilities identified for assessment:

1 Use of apparatus.
2 Make accurate observations.
3 Recognise relationships and draw conclusions.
4 Communicate about experiments.
5 Devise and organise experiments.
6 Solve technological problems.

For the *Single Science Award* or the *Double Science Award* – one overall assessment for each skill is submitted.
Moderation – the internally assessed components will be moderated by inspection by the Examination Group.

4.4 SEG

SCIENCE (SINGLE/DOUBLE)

20% Coursework is to be found in this syllabus that allows for both double and single certification. In the practical assessment 7 objectives have been identified:

1 Devise experiments and select suitable apparatus.
2 Evaluate the design of experiments.
3 Communicate observations, ideas and arguments.
4 Draw conclusions and evaluate critically experimental observations and other data.
5 Carry out practical techniques and procedures.
6 Follow instructions accurately.
7 Observe, measure and record accurately and systematically.

The scale for the award of marks is 3, 2, 1 and 0, and is based on 'can do' descriptions that are provided.
For the *Single Science Award* – assess each assessment objective *twice*.
For the *Double Science Award* – assess each assessment objective *four* times.
Moderation – local standardisation meetings will be held. One teacher from each school to attend and ensure that candidates from the centre are assessed in accordance with the criteria. Written samples will be requested for external moderation by the Examination Group.

INTEGRATED SCIENCE (DOUBLE)

25% Coursework with three objectives defined, but within these there are 24 criteria for assessment:

1 Communication and information skills (6 criteria).
2 Design of experiments (6 criteria).
3 Performance of experiments (12 criteria).

For the *Double Science Award* – each of these criteria will be assessed at least once on a scale of 3, 2, 1, and 0. Performance will be matched to 'can-do' descriptions.
Moderation – teachers who are assessing this coursework will attend area standardisation meetings.

THE SCIENCES – DOUBLE AWARD (MODULAR)

The 20% Coursework will be assessed by the class teacher. Seven practical assessment objectives have been identified starting at objective number ten in the syllabus:

10 Devise experiments and select suitable apparatus with reference to its effective and safe use.
11 Evaluate the design of experiments.
12 Communicate observations, ideas and arguments logically, concisely and in appropriate forms.
13 Draw conclusions from, and evaluate critically, experimental data and other data.
14 Carry out practical techniques, procedures and investigations both based on issued instructions and based on procedures devised by the candidate, with due regard to safety.
15 Follow instructions in connection with experimental and practical procedures.
16 Observe, measure and record accurately and systematically.

For each of the above there is a maximum score of 3 and a minimum of 0. The criteria against which candidate performance must be matched are to be found in the syllabus.

The Examination Group makes the point that the marks submitted should reflect the highest student achievements in a variety of different situations, and that it should be remembered that the students are not being *compared* with each other but against a set of *prescribed criteria*.
For single certification – the candidates should be assessed for each objective at least *twice* during the course.
For double certification – the candidates should be assessed for each objective at least *four* times.
Moderation – one teacher from each centre will be required to attend a local standardisation meeting organised by SEG. Before the meeting, samples of work from all the schools to be represented will have been circulated so that at the meeting a common standard can be agreed. In a large school, standardisation would also be necessary within the science department.

4.5 NISEC

SCIENCE (SINGLE)

The 30% Coursework in this syllabus should be based on both field and laboratory work; it will be assessed by teachers. The coursework assessment scheme is as follows, with weightings shown in brackets:

Selection and Planning a) Selection (1).
b) Planning (1).
Carrying out the Investigation: Approach (2).
Practical Skills a) Following instructions (1).
b) Using apparatus and materials (1).
c) Safety (1).
Collection of data a) Observing (1).
b) Measuring (1).
c) Recording (1).
Concluding, Evaluating and Reporting a) Drawing conclusions (1).
b) Evaluating (1).
c) Reporting (1).

Each of the 13 categories receives a maximum score of 3 and a minimum of 0. Written descriptions of the levels are to be found in the syllabus.
The total mark for each of the *four* coursework assessments is the sum of the best level of achievement attained by the candidate in each coursework category.
This gives a maximum score of 39, which is converted into a *points* score with a maximum of 9 and a minimum of 0.
There must be evidence of coursework across *all* the modules and investigation skills may be assessed in any context. One whole investigation must be carried out in each of the following areas:

core biology	core physics
core chemistry	options

Moderation – this will be external and carried out by NISEC.

4.6 WJEC

SCIENCE (SINGLE/DOUBLE)

20% Coursework which should be carried out during the course. WJEC expect this to be carried out during normal class practical lessons, but small practical tests may be used when necessary. Suggested practical work is to be found detailed in the syllabus. 5 skill areas have been identified:

i) the ability to follow instructions when given orally, in writing or in diagrams;
ii) the ability to select suitable apparatus and use it correctly and safely;
iii) the ability to observe and measure accurately and systematically;
iv) the ability to design and carry out an experiment to solve a given problem;
v) the ability to draw conclusions from experimental observations and data.

Four levels of ability are provided in the form of written descriptors which must be matched to performance. Each skill assessment is scored as on a 0 to 4 scale.
For *Single* and *Double Science Awards* – each ability must be assessed *twice*, on the basis of experiments selected by the teacher for this purpose. Teachers will be asked to supply WJEC with a mark out of a maximum of twenty by the first Tuesday in May of the examination year.
Moderation – practical assessment will be moderated by the Examination Group. Samples of practical work from each school is the current method, but group moderation is being discussed. However, the work of all candidates must be retained for inspection by WJEC should the need arise.

4.7 IGCSE

IGCSE COMBINED SCIENCE (SINGLE/DOUBLE)

20% Optional Practical Assessment. Centres that wish to incorporate this element must gain prior approval of the UCLES. If you are following this syllabus you must discuss practical assessment with your teacher or lecturer.

4.8 Checking out your own Science syllabus

There are six regional Examining Groups and each one produces a variety of GCSE Science syllabuses. For overseas students there is an International GCSE (IGCSE) organised by the University of Cambridge Local Examinations Syndicate. Although you may find useful summary information in Chapter 1, Unit 2.2 and Unit 4, you will need to obtain a *complete* copy of the syllabus you are studying from the appropriate Exam Group. Be sure to get full details of *exactly* which syllabus you are studying from your teacher, lecturer or exams officer, so that you get the correct one. Get the syllabus *number* if you can. Coursework requirements are subject to change so it is equally important to make sure that you *check the latest version* of the syllabus, not an outdated one.

The Examination Group addresses are listed here so that you can write and request an order form to purchase your own copy of the syllabus. You will have to complete the order form and enclose the cost of the syllabus and postage.

London and East Anglian Group (LEAG)
'The Lindens', Lexden Road, Colchester CO3 3RL
Tel: 0206 549595
Midland Examining Group (MEG)
University of Cambridge Local Examinations Syndicate, 1 Hills Road, Cambridge CB1 2EU
Tel: 0223 61111
Northern Examining Association (NEA)
31-33 Springfield Avenue, Harrogate, North Yorkshire HG1 2HW
Tel: 0423 66991
Northern Ireland Schools Examinations Council (NISEC)
42 Beechill Road, Belfast BT8 4RS
Tel: 0232 704666
Southern Examining Group (SEG)
Stag Hill House, Guildford GU2 5XJ
Tel: 0483 503123
Welsh Joint Education Committee (WJEC)
245 Western Avenue, Cardiff CF5 2YX
Tel: 0222 561231
International GCSE (IGCSE)
University of Cambridge Local Examinations Syndicate, 1 Hills Road, Cambridge CB1 2EU
Tel: 0223 61111

UNIT 5 USEFUL BACKGROUND READING

- All About GCSE, Maureen Mobley (Heinemann, 1986)
- Examining GCSE Integrated Science, Stone/Andrews/Williams (Hutchinson Education, 1988)
- Exploring Science Series, Ed. M. Smith (Longman, 1985)
- GCSE Science: Revise Guide, Di Barton (Longman, 1989) (The book you are reading is cross-referenced to this text)
- GCSE: A Guide for Parents, Employers and Candidates, G. Gorman (Kogan Page, 1988)
- GCSE: Parent's Guide, A Matten (Northcote House, 1988)
- General Certificate of Education: A General Introduction (HMSO, London 1985)
- Nuffield Co-ordinated Science Series (Longman, 1988)
- Science for Life (Collins 1984)
- Science to Sixteen, Pople/Williams (Oxford, 1987)
- Science GCSE: A Guide for Teachers (SEC/OU, 1986)
- Suffolk Co-ordinated Science Series (Collins, 1987)
- Teaching GCSE Science, P. Dawson (Hodder and Stoughton, 1987)

SUMMARY

1 Find out which Science syllabus you are following.
2 Check the syllabus number and date.
3 Order a copy for yourself.
4 Check out the coursework requirements.
5 Find out what you are doing next and always prepare for lessons.
6 Background reading is useful; make sure you get a suitable text.

CHAPTER 2

TEACHER-ORGANISED SCIENCE COURSEWORK

UNIT 1 TEACHER-DIRECTED ASSESSMENT

This chapter focuses on those skills needed for success in practicals organised by the *teacher*, though many of them are just as essential in student-organised practical work, which is the theme for Chapter 3. This chapter contains good advice which you will need to consider, along with the special requirements of your own syllabus.

Most of the science coursework you do is likely to have been planned and organised by your teacher, or by the science department in your school or college. Usually there will be obvious and important links between the practical coursework you do and the theory you have studied for that topic. In Chapter 4, each example of coursework has been put under the *topic area* to which it belongs.

In some science courses, such as Suffolk Co-ordinated Science, 'Can-do tests' are used to assess certain skills and abilities, including *manipulative tasks*, such as 'using apparatus and measuring instruments'. Some of these tests are built into each unit of work. Success or failure is obvious in activities such as using a 'newtonmeter' or 'focusing a microscope'. Such activities can often fit into the normal pattern of working, and do not require special tests. They should be looked upon as confidence builders, that is to say milestones on the road to success.

Always remember that your teacher *wants* you to succeed. Don't be afraid to ask for help if you need it. You will not usually be assessed in a particular skill until you are ready.

UNIT 2 FOLLOWING INSTRUCTIONS

This should be an area for scoring high marks. You will be given a set of instructions which will tell you how to carry out an experiment. These instructions will be written, spoken, or in the form of diagrams/flow charts.

Your role is to *follow* the instructions as closely as possible. While this sounds simple, success relies on having a **very clear understanding** of the actual instructions. The skills you need to use are slightly different for the different types of instructions, so these have been treated separately.

2.1 Spoken instructions and/or demonstrations

In some ways *spoken* instructions are the easiest, because you can ask questions during the instructions. However, there are a few ways you can help yourself.

GET AN OVERVIEW

Find out as soon as possible what the experiment is about. Usually it will relate to the *topic* you are studying. It may be possible from your knowledge of that topic to work out what you have to do in your own mind. If you can do this it will make it easier to see *why* different steps have to be carried out.

GET A GOOD VIEW

Preferably not by fighting your way to the front! Your teacher will want to make sure that *everyone* can see properly. You will be able to succeed without spoiling the chances of others.

LISTEN CAREFULLY

Remember that you will have to follow the instructions exactly, so listen carefully. If something does not make sense, or if you find yourself thinking 'why was that done?', then ask. Hopefully you will be given a reason that will help you to understand.

WATCH CAREFULLY

This is especially important if the apparatus is complicatd or difficult to set up. Take care to notice the *order* of assembly as a step-by-step sequence of events. This will help you to set the apparatus up when it is your turn.

MAKE NOTES

Making notes will help, especially if the experiment is long. Be sure your notes include *all* the important details, such as how much of each reagent was used (how many drops or cm^3 or gms?).

List the steps in order and *number them* to give them a logical sequence. *Sketching* the apparatus may help, both at this stage and when it comes to writing the experiment up.

ASK QUESTIONS

The right time to ask questions is usually *during the explanation*. Get a clear idea of the method you need to use before the explanation is finished. Remember, the only stupid question is the one that was *not* asked!

CHECK THE APPARATUS

Sometimes even the best-planned practical sessions are not perfect. If your instructions tell you to use an item of apparatus which you are sure is not there, then ask about it. But do so *before* you get started on the practical.

2.2 Written instructions

The instructions may be written, as in Fig 2.1, page 18. The aim is just the same, but the method you use is obviously different with *written* instructions. It basically boils down to accurate reading. For a few people this is no problem, but most would benefit from the following approach:

- **Step by step instructions**
  Here the instructions are already written out rather like a recipe. This should help make the instructions easier to follow, as long as you do not 'lose your place'. Tick off each completed instruction.
- **Prose instructions**
  Sometimes the instructions will be written out in lengthy paragraphs. These should be converted into a *point by point check list*, as above. This can be very brief, as it is for your use only. Again, tick off as you complete the tasks.

READ THE INSTRUCTIONS CAREFULLY

Most instructions refer to *apparatus*. If you are not certain which piece is which, then it is worth *picking up* each piece of apparatus as you read through. This will be useful when there are similar devices to use, such as different resistors, voltmeters or ammeters. If *solutions* are mentioned, make sure you know which type each one is. It is much easier to use the correct solution if you already have a mental image of Benedict's solution as 'the blue liquid' and iodine solution as 'the brown liquid'. Where possible also use colours to distinguish between *chemicals*. If chemicals are the same colour, then make a mental note to read the label carefully.

CHECK THE APPARATUS

Make sure you have everything you will need. Do so at the *start*, nothing is worse than getting half way through and then finding that something is missing.

SAMPLE WORKSHEET — EXCRETION

WHAT'S IN URINE?

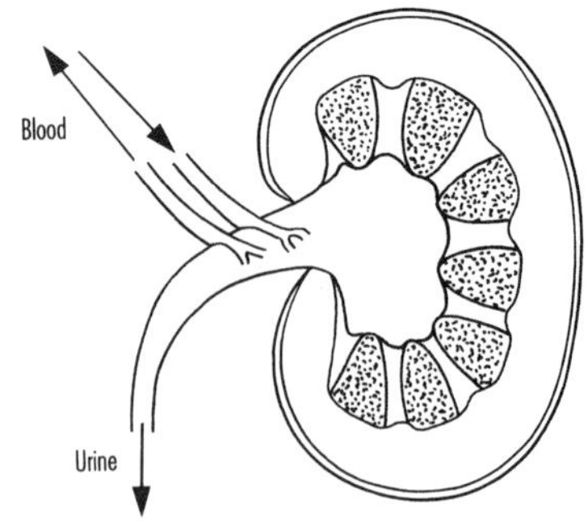

Test the two samples of urine to see if they contain:

Salt (sodium chloride)
Urea
Sugar
Starch

You will find the *tests for starch and glucose* in your work on nutrition.

To test for salt: add a few drops of **silver nitrate** to two cm depth of the urine in a test tube. A whitish colour shows the presence of chloride ions, and therefore shows that there is salt in the urine.

To test for urea do the Biuret test as follows: Add about 1 cm of **sodium hydroxide** to 2 cm depth of the sample. Follow this by pouring a few drops of copper sulphate down the side of the test tube. A purplish colour shows the presence of urea. If this is not seen immediately, shake the tube gently and then observe.

For each of your tests:
Choose your apparatus carefully.
Draw a diagram to show what you did.
Record ALL observations.

After you have done your tests: leave your test tubes with the chemicals in so that your teacher can look at them.

Which of the samples of urine is likely to have come from a person who is ill? Say why.

Fig 2.1
Sample worksheet: urine testing

CHECK YOUR UNDERSTANDING

Be ruthless with yourself. Make sure you know what you are going to do before starting. Ask yourself – 'do I know what this experiment is investigating/showing/trying to prove?' If the answer is 'no' then go back to the written instructions, and work through them again, this time more slowly. Aim to check every detail when you do this; there is usually one small part of the instruction which causes problems.

If you are still stuck, ask for help with the instructions. It is better to do this at the beginning. Asking for help may affect your mark, but far less than by going ahead and making mistakes later.

2.3 Diagrams and flow-charts

These are widely used, and are often used in combination with other forms of instruction. You will need to be sure that you know, and can recognise, diagrams of the common pieces of laboratory apparatus. In Fig 2.2 you will first see a *drawing* (labelled a)) and then the accepted *diagrammatic representation* (labelled b)) of each item of laboratory equipment.

Fig 2.2
Common laboratory apparatus

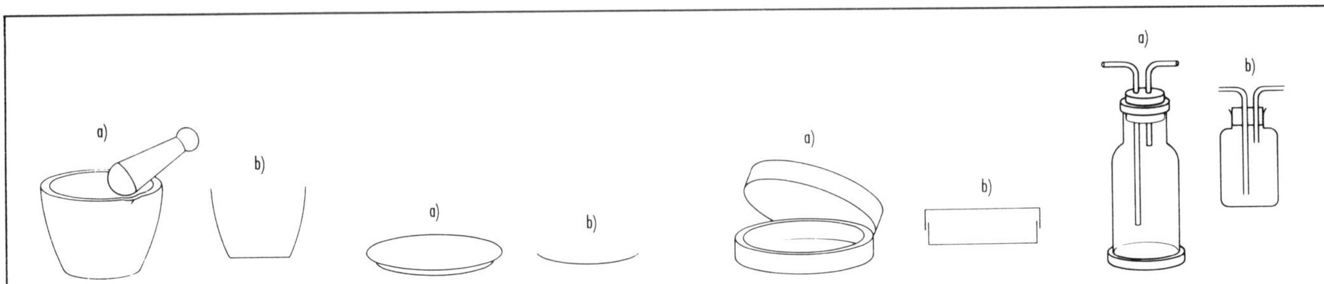

Pestle and mortar
Used for grinding up substances.

Clock glass
Used for evaporating a small amount of solution.

Petri dish
Used for cultivating micro-organisms.

Gas-washing bottle (Dreschel bottle)
Used for passing gas through a liquid.

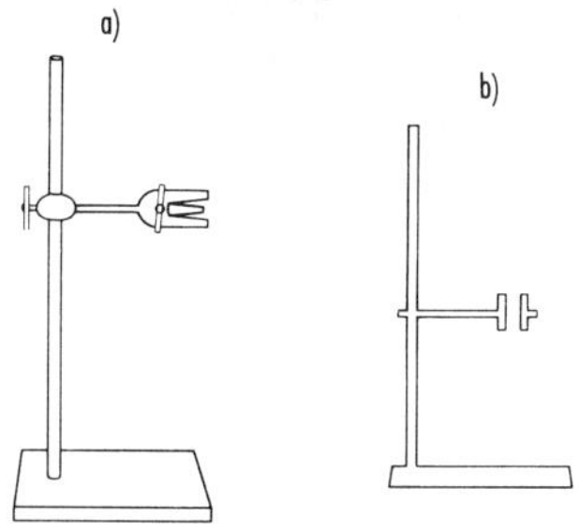

Retort stand and clamp
Used for holding objects in position.

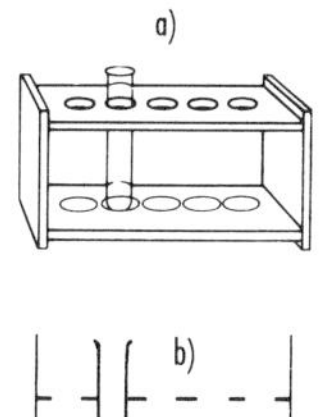

Test tube rack
Used for holding test tubes and boiling tubes.

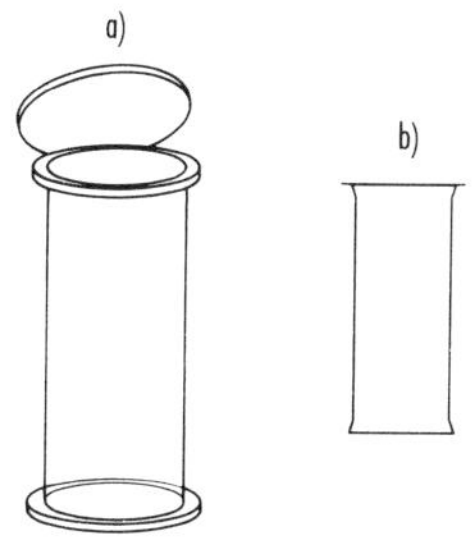

Gas Jar and cover
Used for holding gases.

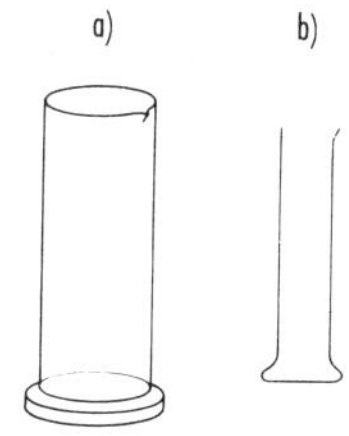

Graduated cylinder
Used for delivering an approximate volume of liquid.

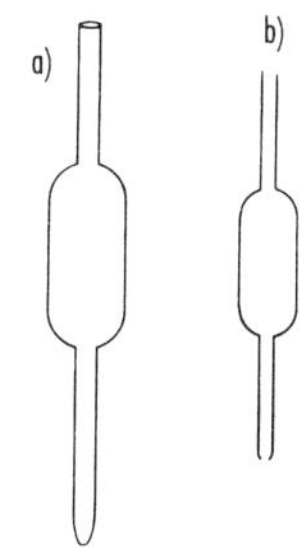

Pipette
Used for delivering a fixed volume of liquid.

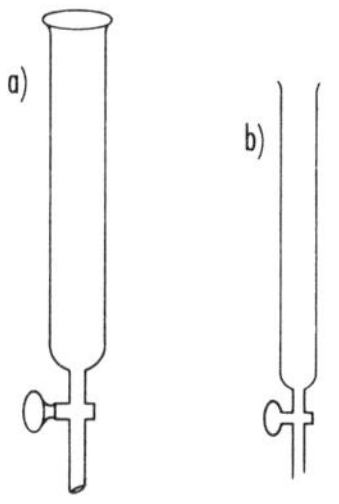

Burette
Used for delivering an accurate volume of liquid (0 to 50 cm^3)

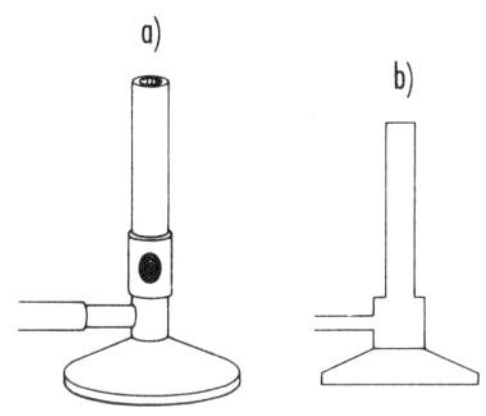

Bunsen burner
Used for heating.

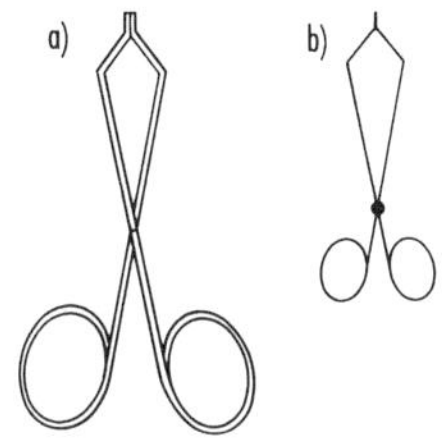

Tongs
Used for holding objects (particularly if hot).

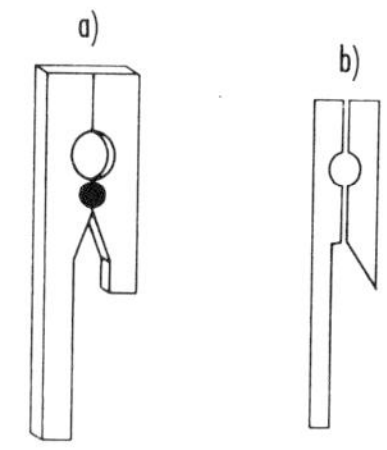

Test tube holder
Used for holding test tube or boiling tube.

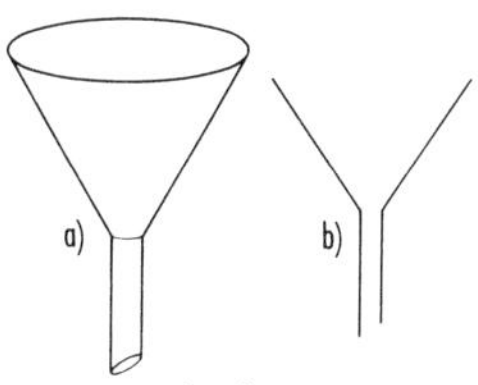

Funnel
Used for filling burette, filtering (with aid of filter paper), etc.

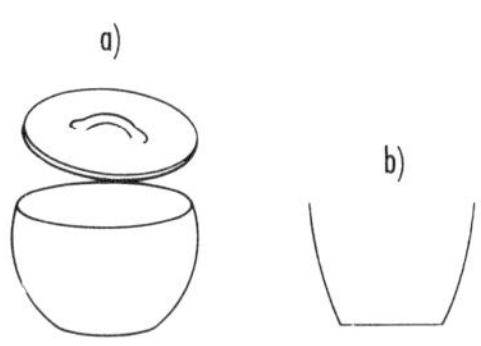

Crucible
Used for heating solids to a high temperature.

Evaporating basin
Used for evaporating a solution.

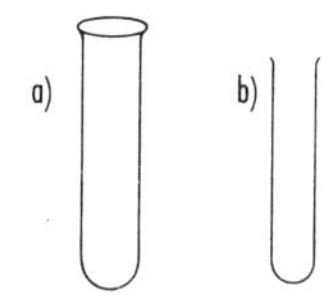

Test tube
Used for heating solids or liquids.

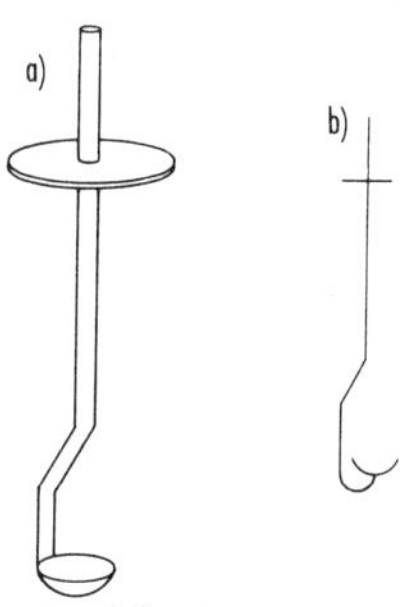

Deflagrating spoon
(combustion spoon)
Used for burning substances in a gas.

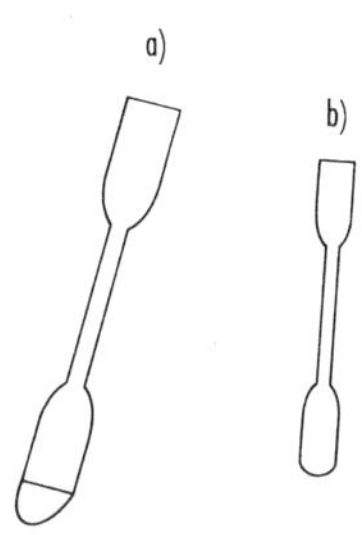

Spatula
Used for picking up a small quantity of a solid.

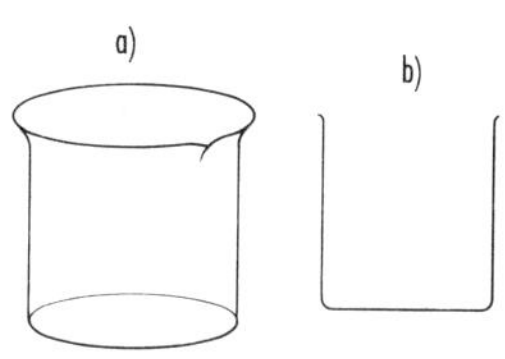

Beaker
Used for holding liquids.

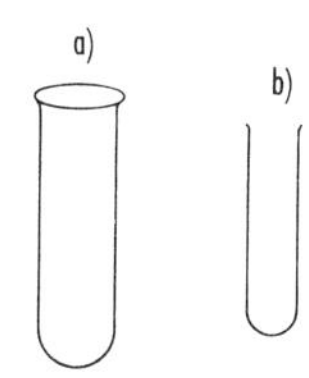

Boiling tube
Used for holding solids and liquids.

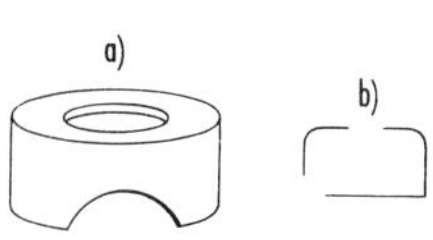

Bee-hive shelf
Used when collecting a gas over water.

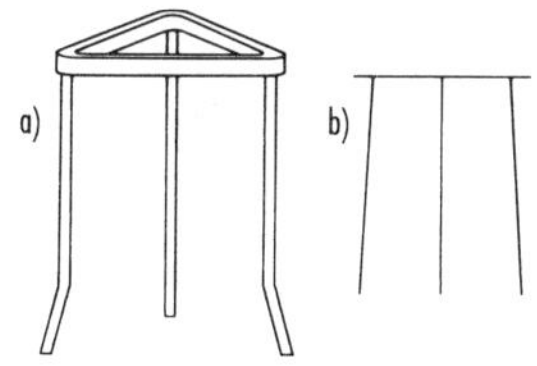

Tripod
Used for supporting wire gauze or pipe-clay triangle.

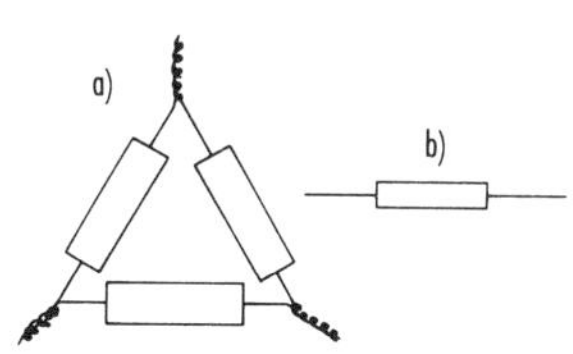

Pipe-clay triangle
Used for supporting crucible.

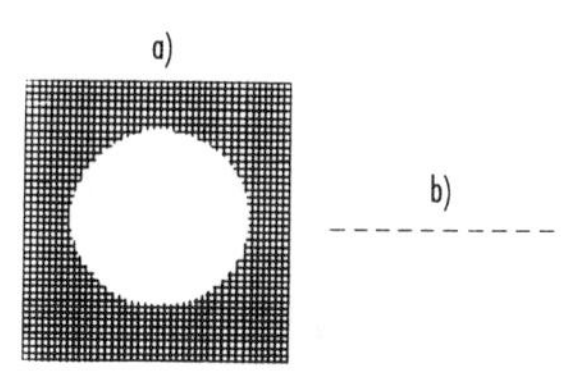

Wire gauze
Used to spread heat when heating a flask or beaker.

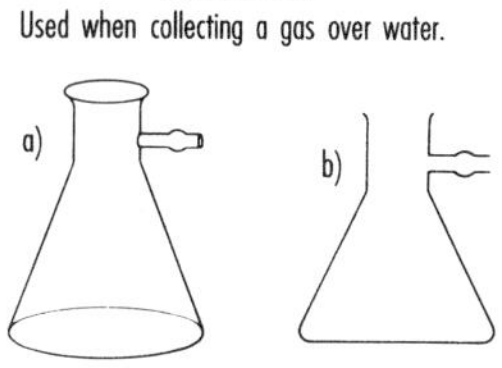

Buchner flask
Used in preparation of gases and for filtering under suction.

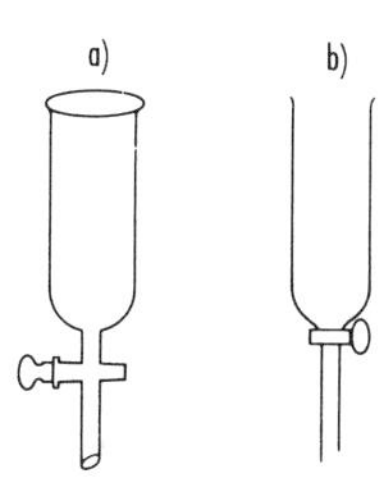

Separating funnel or dropping funnel
Used for separating liquids or adding a liquid to a flask.

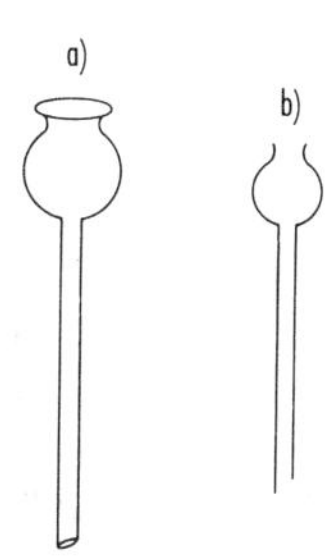

Thistle funnel
Used for adding a liquid to a flask.

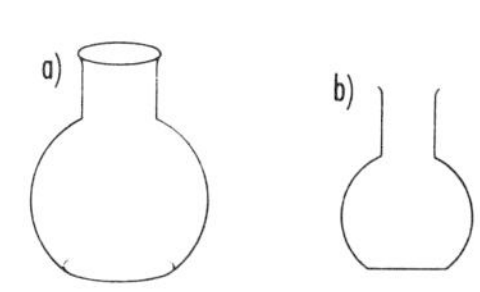

Flat bottomed flask
Used for holding liquids.

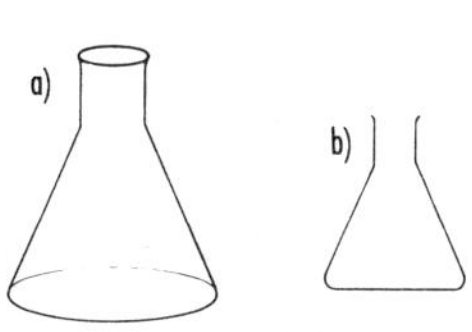

Conical flask
Used for holding liquids.

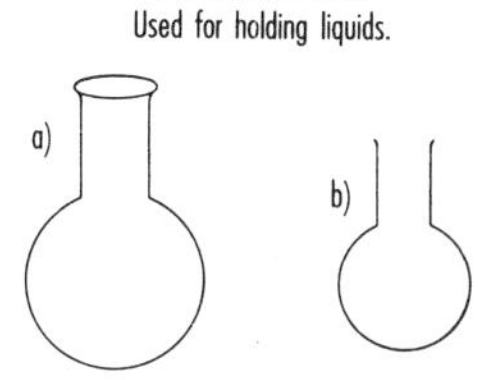

Round bottomed flask
Used for heating liquids.

The *flow diagram* shown in Fig 2.3 uses a style something between a drawing and a correct symbol. This is a style *not* to be copied! It does however give very clear instructions, but, danger lurks! Look at picture 3 – a flame is shown near to boiling alcohol! Never! Always be safety conscious!

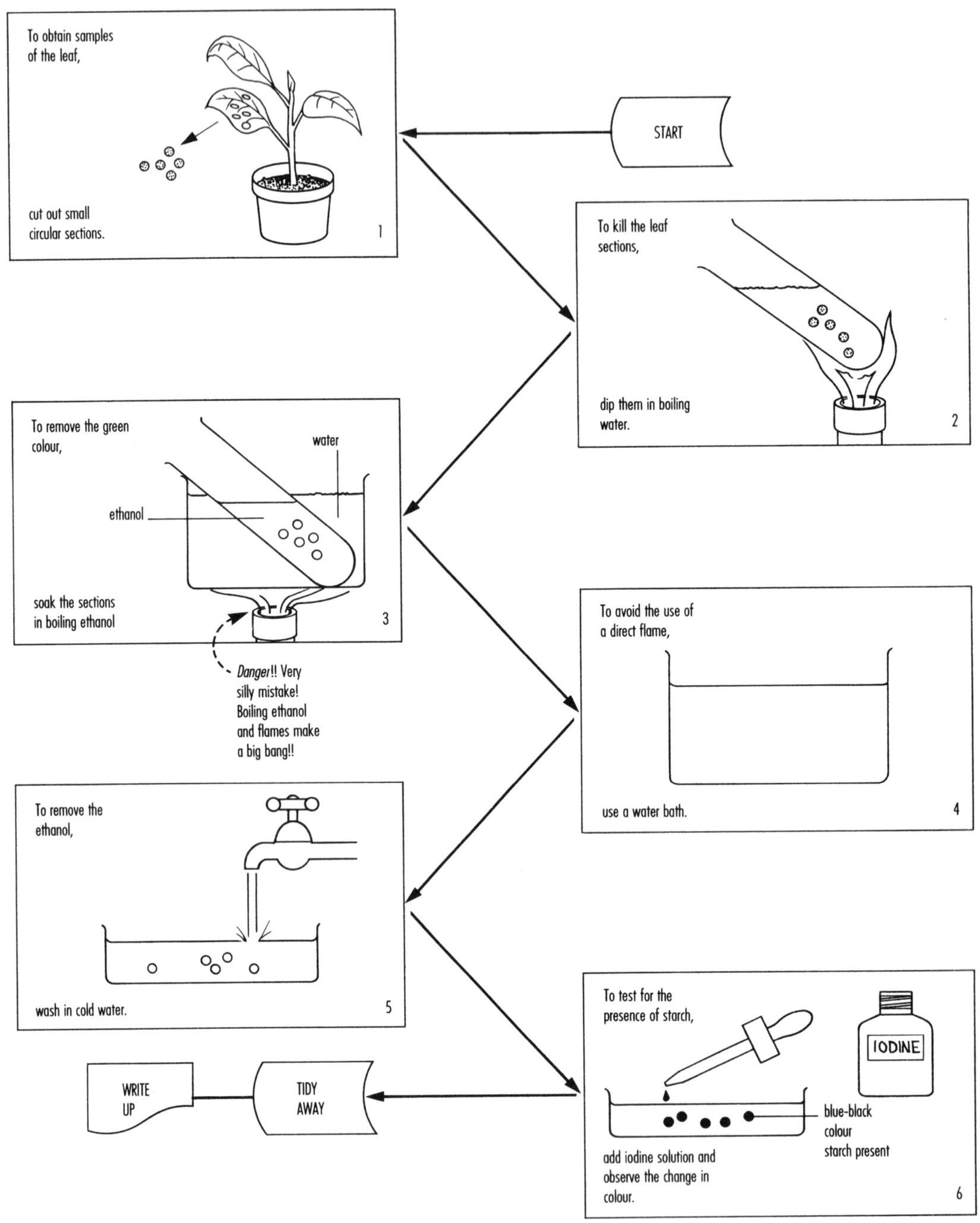

Fig 2.3
Flow diagram: testing a leaf for starch

Electrical circuit diagrams are common in practical science and there are special symbols for all the components. You would be wise to learn them as you use them. Most are shown in Fig 2.4. Building *circuits* from diagrams is fun, when you know what you are doing and particularly if they behave as you expect when they are 'powered up'. In Fig 2.5 a) and b) on page 22 there are some questions to test your understanding of circuits.

There are many symbols in chemistry too; each *element* can be written as a symbol, and so can *compounds*. Learn these as you study; try keeping your own 'dictionary' of chemical symbols on a sheet of A4 paper in your file. Add each new element or compound as you meet it.

Perhaps the most important symbols are those concerned with safety, or usually the opposite – **DANGER**. These are dealt with in Unit 3 of this chapter.

Fig 2.4
Electrical and electronic symbols

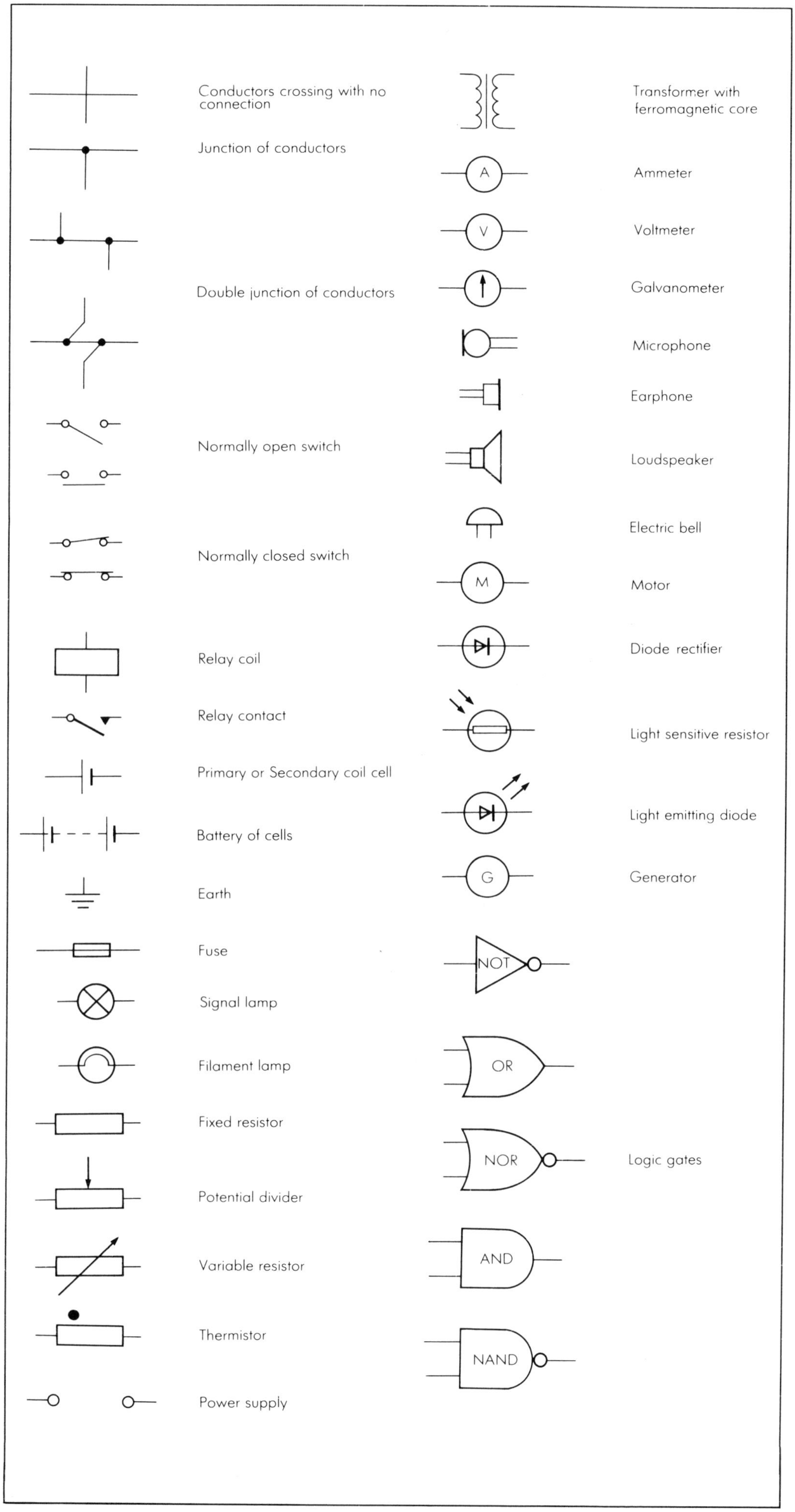

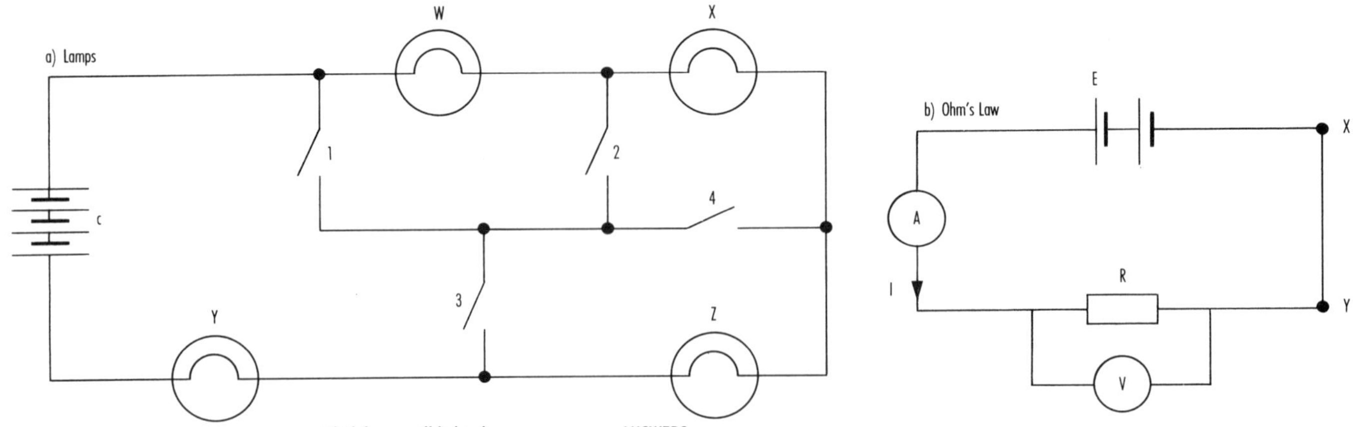

Fig 2.5
Circuit diagrams

Which lamps will light when:	ANSWERS
the circuit is as shown above?	
only switch 1 is closed?	
only switch 2 is closed?	
only switch 3 is closed?	
only switch 4 is closed?	
switches 1 and 2 are closed?	
switches 1 and 3 are closed?	
switches 1 and 4 are closed?	
switches 2 and 3 are closed?	
switches 2 and 4 are closed?	
switches 3 and 4 are closed?	
switches 1, 2 and 3 are closed?	
switches 1, 2 and 4 are closed?	
switches 2, 3 and 4 are closed?	
all the switches are closed?	

QUESTIONS		MARKS
1	Which units are used to measure E?	*(1)*
2	Which units are used to measure I?	*(1)*
3	Which units are used to measure V?	*(1)*
4	Which units are used to measure R?	*(1)*
5	What is the relationship between, V, I and R?	*(1)*
6	How is the ammeter connected?	*(1)*
7	Comment on the resistance of the ammeter.	*(1)*
8	How is the voltmeter connected?	*(1)*
9	Comment on the resistance of the voltmeter.	*(1)*
10	What value would you expect a voltmeter to read if connected across X and Y?	*(1)*

2.4 How marks are awarded

Having a clear idea what the instructions *mean* is one thing. However, you will be graded on what you actually *did*. This may mean more than just 'following the recipe'. Most of the mark schemes give credit for simply following instructions, but top marks are sometimes only available to those who have done a bit more. For example, if there are 6 marks for an assessment on following instructions, they could be awarded as follows:

- **For 2 marks** – 'Student has followed instructions to perform a single practical operation without assistance'.

This might mean successfully making one measurement, or carrying out a single food test. Note the 'without assistance'. This is why you must get clear understanding *before* starting. If you need to ask during the experiment, then you have not shown that you can follow the instructions.

- **For 4 marks** – 'Student has followed a series of step-by-step instructions successfully'.

The difference here is that the operation carried out is more complex. This might involve setting up a circuit and using it to make several measurements, or carrying out a chemical reaction and testing the products. Some of the experiments carried out will be of this sort. Note that the highest possible mark is 4. Usually you can get this mark by 'recipe following'.

Some syllabuses use the *amount of help* you need to decide how many marks you get; for 3 out of 4 marks you may have succeeded, but with lots of help. On this 'help' system of marking, you would be allowed a little help or one mistake in the experiment (e.g. *one* wrong reading) without any penalty.

- **For 6 marks** – 'Student has followed complex instructions to perform a series of operations in which the later ones may have to be altered because of earlier results'.

This is where your understanding of the *point* of the experiment comes into play. By knowing what the experiment is trying to illustrate, it will be easier to alter the later steps. If you find that an experiment gives results which are *not* as you would expect, then there are two options.

Firstly, think back; did you do everything correctly? Were the steps in the correct order? Were the amounts and types of reagents correct? If in doubt, *repeat* the exercise.

Secondly, if the result is the same, then try to work out *why* it is unusual. Perhaps you should dilute one of the solutions; or check your wiring or your measurements.

Suppose you are asked to identify the nutrients in an onion. Your instructions tell you how to test for protein, lipid, starch, reducing sugar and non-reducing sugar. You find that it has reducing sugar in it. Do you then go ahead and test for non-reducing sugar? No, because the test you have been given will not detect it if there is reducing sugar present. So you have had to *alter* one of the later stages because of an earlier result. For that you would get 6 marks.

2.5 Coursework requiring these skills

In any practical exercise during your science course you are likely to be following instructions of some sort, to a lesser or greater degree. All the examples in this book (see also Chapter 1, Unit 3.1 and Chapter 4, Units 1-13) include instructions; think them through as you read the examples. Your teacher could assess this skill on almost any occasion; remember the good advice in this chapter and be ready.

UNIT 3

APPARATUS AND MATERIALS

“Selecting the apparatus involves good judgement.”

Following instructions occasionally requires you to use your *judgement* in order to gain the highest marks. When assessment is carried out on your ability to select and use apparatus, your judgement is the first skill that comes into play. When you select apparatus you are making a judgement. That judgement is important, since it affects *how well* you can actually do the experiment. Really, the only way to develop judgement is through experience and regular practice.

Before looking at ways of *handling* the apparatus, there are a few points to bear in mind. If you think of someone you know who is 'good at experiments', and then ask yourself what they are like you'll probably come up with a list of words which included such things as 'involved', 'busy', 'organised' or perhaps even 'bossy'.

In a lot of science classes these days there is a need to work in *groups*. Within every group there will be some people who *do more* than others. Another way of looking at this is that there are some people who get *more practice* with the apparatus than others. Very often they are the same ones who are 'good at experiments'. If **you** are the one who organises the others, then this introduction is *not* written for you. If, however, you tend to let the others do the work while you stand back, then it most certainly is! Think hard, when it comes to the assessment, who will have the better chance of success?

Basically, you must make sure that your chance of practical experience is not spoiled by others. Even if at times you are not able to *use* the apparatus, you can still find out *how* it works, so that you are ready in case you are the one who has to perform during the assessment!

Let's now have a look at the different aspects that make up this skill of handling apparatus effectively.

3.1 How to handle common apparatus

Any list of 'common' apparatus would include the following (see also Fig 2.2 above):

“Some common items of apparatus.”

- bunsen burner
- boiling tube
- stop watch
- measuring cylinders
- electrical meters
- thermometers (yes, you would be surprised how many people still remove them from the liquid to read!)
- hand lens
- microscope
- safety goggles

Remember, you should be able to use all these **accurately**, **safely** and **independently**, even when you have just had games and you've only just got your breath back. In other words, you must be so familiar with these that you do not have to think about how to use them.

At the same time you must always be careful. Many people get nervous when being assessed on this skill, since it often involves being closely watched by the teacher. Try not to be. It may help to remember that most GCSE Science schemes allow you to be assessed **at least twice** in most areas of skill. If you make a mess of things the first time, there should be more than one chance to show what you can really do. Learn from your mistakes and let your teacher know that you intend to!

3.2 How to handle chemicals

The key thought to have in mind is that any *chemical* you use (including water) may be dangerous in some way. Once again your use must involve the greatest possible care. The most commonly used 'dangerous' chemicals in Science are **acids** and **alkalis**. Both of these are corrosive, and will cause damage to your skin. Some **enzymes** used in schools are also dangerous. If you have an accident or spillage with any of these the safety rules are simple:

1 Wash the chemical off with **lots** of water.
2 **Report** the accident to your teacher.

With other chemicals you use it is important to find out what kind of hazard they might present, and to know how to deal with them if an accident does occur. Your teacher or lecturer will almost always warn you if there is potential danger, but you must read instructions thoroughly, noting any warnings given. Do look at the labels on the containers. There are international symbols for chemical hazards, and these are shown in Fig 2.6. It is *your* job to make sure you get information about chemicals before you start to use them.

Fig 2.6 Hazard symbols

You will also get credit for making sure that your bench does not accumulate even the smallest 'puddle' or 'pile' of any chemical. Spillages present a danger to you and to other laboratory users, including your teacher.

Use small or stated amounts of any chemicals provided. Often small quantities give faster and better results. For instance 'indicators', such as 'Universal Indicator', are often incorrectly used, as when students use so much of them that the all-important colour change is not at all obvious.

3.3 How to handle biological material

The term 'biological material' can include a very wide variety of things. These may be grouped as follows:

LIVING ORGANISMS

Living organisms include microbes (bacteria or yeast cells), invertebrate animals (woodlice, earthworms or maggots), small vertebrates (mice) and plants (algae, small flowering plants). Often living organisms are studied in the place where they actually live; such work is called *ecology*. Whenever you are given the chance to work 'in the field' you must remember to cause as little change as possible. There are two reasons for this. Firstly, there will be other students studying that area later, and you will not help them if you harm anything. Secondly, there is an unwritten law that scientists have a responsibility for *any* living thing they are studying. The later section on ecology explains this more fully.

DEAD ORGANISMS OR PARTS OF ORGANISMS

These are often preserved specimens in jars of fluid, or things like bones, teeth, flowers, leaves and twigs. Your aim, when dealing with these, is to be as gentle as possible. The organisms in the jars are often quite fragile, and shaking them up will not make them any easier to observe.

FRESH MATERIAL

This could include fluids such as saliva, but many Local Education Authorities have stopped the use of blood and cheek cells due to the risks of HIV infection. Many schools and colleges offer students the chance to look at various organs from animals like sheep or cows. Whenever you handle anything biological, especially if it comes from an animal, make sure you always wash your hands thoroughly afterwards. Similarly, the bench you have been working on should be cleaned properly to prevent microbes or animal remains affecting others. There is a slight health risk when working with this kind of material, but it can be removed by care and by attention to simple hygiene.

The GCSE criteria state that you cannot be **required** to take part in, or even to watch, any dissection of animals or parts of animals. If you do *not* wish to take part, tell the teacher in advance. Most teachers would not base an important assessment on this kind of work, and are usually understanding when students ask to opt out.

3.4 How marks are awarded

As with all the assessments, the marks are awarded for the different abilities shown. Once again, most marks are available for the most organised approach, particularly if it occurs in a complicated situation. Since some of the Exam Groups use a 6 as the best possible mark, the examples shown will take this as the top mark.

For the Exam Groups which test the ability to handle apparatus and materials independently, the teachers are asked to check the following kinds of things:

- 2 marks – 'Uses familiar apparatus and materials adequately, needing reminders on points of safety.'
- 4 marks – 'The student uses familiar apparatus, materials and techniques adequately and safely.'
- 6 marks – 'Uses familiar apparatus, materials and techniques safely, correctly and methodically.'

Looking at these statements, it becomes clearer what is involved. To make sure you get more than 2 marks, you must work **SAFELY**. But to get full marks you need to show that you can work **METHODICALLY**. Once again the key lies in *organisation*. To be methodical, you need to be able to concentrate on the task in front of you. So make sure you have everything you will need in terms of pencils, ruler, etc. Also make sure you have a full understanding of the task.

For marking these tasks, many teachers use 'check lists'. These lists detail *particular things* that your teacher is watching for. You score for each thing you do properly. Some typical checklist items are:

- Apparatus checked before starting.
- Goggles worn whilst heating.
- Goggles worn when handling dangerous chemicals.
- Careful handling of acid/alkali/peroxide.
- Labelled tubes/containers correctly.
- Correct amounts of reagents used.
- Apparatus not too near edge of bench.

It is not a good idea to try to work out what is on your teacher's list. It is far better to rely on your *own ability* to do the job properly.

3.5 Coursework requiring these skills

There are so many ways that are used to assess these particular skills that any list could only cover a limited range of possibilities. You can assume that *any* experiment you do could be part of an assessment in this area. Indeed the points made here apply to any practical work you carry out.

SUMMARY

1 During normal laboratory work, GET SOME PRACTICE.
2 ORGANISE and SUCCEED.
3 CARE, SAFETY and RESPECT FOR LIFE.
4 CHEMICALS are DANGEROUS.
5 RELY ON YOUR OWN ABILITY.
6 NOT TOO NEAR THE EDGE.

UNIT 4 OBSERVING AND MEASURING

When the early discoveries were made in science, they were usually made by people described as **observers**. These people were usually interested 'amateurs' who happened to notice something that caught their interest. They then often tried to repeat the circumstances that led to their observation, and thus carried out *experiments*.

When experimenting, the observers were often looking for *particular things* to check whether their first observations were accurate. In other words, they judged **relevance**. When they recorded their results, they only wrote down **relevant** information.

Try to work out the aim of the experiment. This will help you decide what information is relevant and therefore worth recording.

If you are being assessed on your ability to observe and measure, it will be important that you record **only the essential** (relevant) **information**. You can judge what this is by having a clear idea of the point of the experiment. Knowing *what* you are looking for is the first step in making good observations. If you have any doubt about what you are trying to achieve, then try to state the **aim** of the experiment as a question.

Suppose, for example, you are using different-sized blocks of limestone with hydrochloric acid, and then timing how long it takes to fill up a boiling tube with carbon dioxide. In this case your aim might be stated as follows:

- How does particle size affect the rate of a reaction? (See also Chapter 3, Unit 4.2) In this case, you need observations, or measurements, of:

  a) the dimensions of the blocks
  b) the time taken to fill the boiling tubes.

It is easy in this case to list 'pointless' observations and measurements. But what about recording the *temperature*! Temperature can affect the *rate* of reaction. If temperature changes during the experiment, then it may affect your results. In this case you should, if possible, measure the temperature as well.

The apparatus may give you a clue on what to measure.

In many experiments you can judge which things to measure by the *apparatus* you are given.

4.1 Qualitative observations

These are *observations* and not measurements. They could include work on the following areas:

COLOUR DIFFERENCES

Examples include differences between a destarched leaf and a normal leaf when testing with iodine solution; or between different results for a Benedict's test on different strengths of glucose solution. Many chemical reactions involve changes in colour.

STRUCTURAL DIFFERENCES

Examples include differences between types of bones, or microscope slides, or types of crystal, or types of pulley system.

REACTION DIFFERENCES

Examples include observations to detect whether a gas is evolved when different chemicals are reacted with acids, or whether a gas will support burning. (**Hint**: If you are not sure whether or not a solution is giving off a gas, then **listen very carefully** to the end of the test tube; but remember that acids will not improve the hearing!)

In essence, observing is not a difficult skill – the difficulty comes in judging the relevant things to record. Remember that you will usually be judged on what you write down, so make sure you record **AT LEAST** the observations you are asked for.

At times you will be asked to record observations as *drawings* and *diagrams*. There are particular rules for these graphic communications which should be kept in mind:

Important rules for drawings and diagrams.

1. **Neatness** often equals **Marks**.
2. **Pencil** for **Drawing**, **Ink** for **Labels**.
3. **Scale** is **Important**.
4. **Apparatus** should be drawn as a **Two-dimensional** 'slice'.
5. **Liquid levels** should be **Horizontal**.

6 **Circuit** symbols should be **used** when appropriate.
7 **Colours** should not normally be used.
8 When drawing **Apparatus**, use a **Ruler**.

When drawing anything living **DO NOT** use a ruler – if you wonder why, just look at the 'straightest' part of any living thing, and you will see that it is not 'ruler-straight'. One very frequent mistake involves drawings of plant cells from 'onion skin' (epidermis). While these are described as 'brick-like', you will lose credit for drawing what could easily be assumed to be a brick wall!

Use of technology to gather data

4.2 Quantitative observations

These are *measurements*. The important rules to bear in mind are as follows:

UNITS

Whenever you measure something, make sure you write down the *units*. If the result is going into a table, the unit should be at the top, as part of the column heading (see later section on recording).

ACCURACY

Your measurements should be as accurate as possible **within the limits of your apparatus**. In other words, there is no point in using a ruler which has *centimetres* as the smallest division and then 'guessing' the *millimetres* in your measurement. There is a point beyond which you cannot go in terms of accuracy. Again, suppose you are asked to measure approximately 50 cm^3 of soil, as part of an experiment to find out how much air there is in it. You are not allowed to compress the soil, and you find that there is 49.5 cm^3 in your measuring cylinder. There would be no point in this case of trying to be any more accurate.

The different Exam Groups require different degrees of accuracy with the various instruments. You should try to find out what degree of accuracy is required by *your* exam group. Asking your teacher should provide the answer.

Temperature

Some groups require temperature to be measured to the nearest degree Celsius (°C), while for others it must be to the nearest half a degree. For most students this will involve the laboratory thermometer, and very occasionally clinical thermometers, electronic temperature gauges or thermocouples. Whichever instrument you use, make sure you know how to operate it effectively. If in doubt, ask for help!

Time

This usually involves measurement in seconds to the nearest second. The *second* is the standard scientific unit of time. In this case there is a need to bear in mind the required accuracy. Suppose you have a stop watch that measures to the nearest 1/100 s and you are timing a reaction that takes 90 s, you may find that your watch states 89.82 s. When you record the result, round it up to the nearest second, which would of course be 90 s.

Mass

Electronic top pan balances are increasingly being used in schools and colleges. When you have to use one of these, make sure that it reads zero before you start weighing. This may involve using a 'tare' button or 'reset zero'. If you are not sure that the instrument is performing correctly, ask your teacher, rather than risking damage to an expensive device. Remember to take the mass of the *container* into account. This may be possible without writing anything down; if not, make sure you write down what each measurement stands for. If you are weighing objects which are hot or wet, they should not be placed directly onto the pan of the balance. Similarly, chemicals should be weighed in a container, or on some filter paper.

A triple-beam balance in use

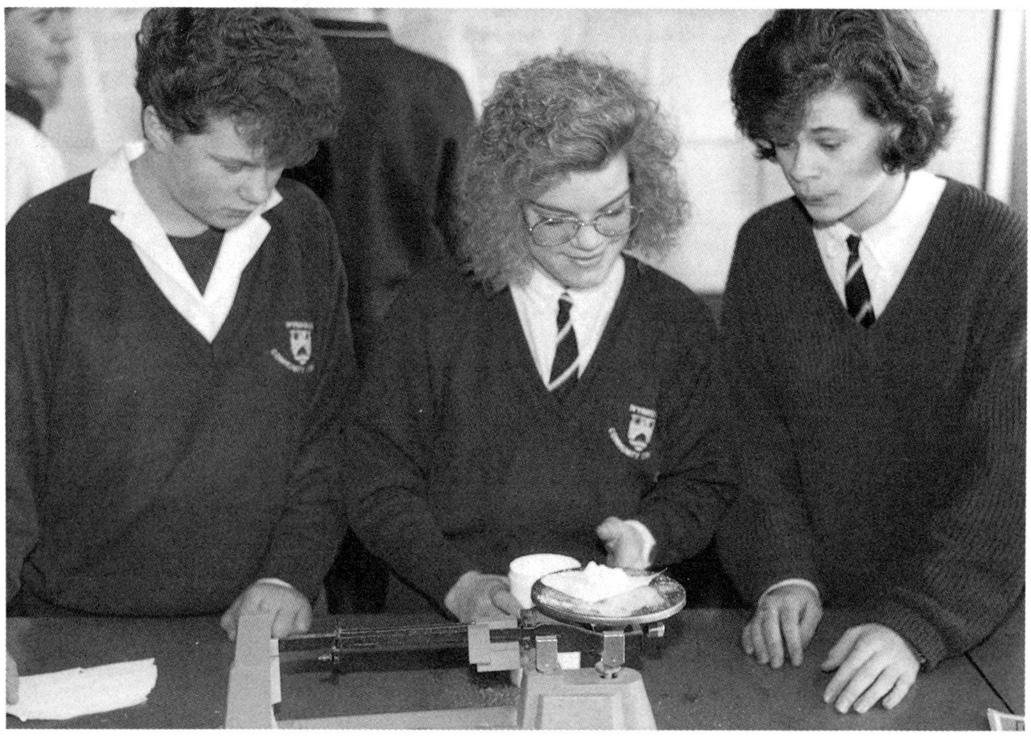

Length

In measuring any length, you must look **straight** down at right angles to the ruler and the object. Failure to do so will make the measurements inaccurate due to **parallax** error. The units for any length measurement will be determined by the size of the object being measured. Generally speaking, if you can measure something to within 1/200 (0.5%) of its total length, you are about right. This means that if you are measuring a wire approximately 1m long, the length can be expressed to the nearest 0.5cm. There will be many times when this is not possible (e.g. changes in lengths of potato chips during an investigation into diffusion or osmosis), in which case you are limited to the accuracy of your ruler. It is **never** worth trying to achieve greater accuracy than to the nearest mm, unless you are using special instruments such as a 'micrometer' or a special 'graticule' (a microscope slide with very accurate measurements engraved on it!) during microscope work.

“Round up or down after you have made your calculations.”

Volume

This is most often measured using measuring cylinders. Remember to read at the **bottom of the meniscus**. Sometimes, although you may use a syringe, the same rule applies. At other times you will have to work out volumes of regular cubes using the standard *length* × *width* ×

Co-operation: pouring carefully

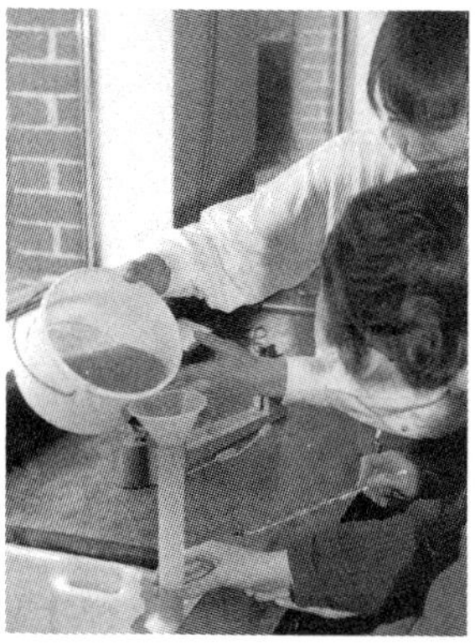

height formula. When this is the case, make sure you measure accurately, since the calculation itself will exaggerate any tiny errors. Suppose you end up with a volume which reads as 29.7825 cm^3. If you wrote that down as the volume, the question would be asked – 'How can you be so accurate?' In this case, the correct thing to do is to write down your measurements, then make your calculations, and only **at the end** to convert the volume to the nearest whole number. In our case, 29.8 cm^3 or 30.0 cm^3 might be more realistic for the rounded figure.

4.3 How marks are awarded

For *quantitative* observations, the marks are simply awarded for appropriately accurate measurements. This is when previous practice with the apparatus will come in useful.

Marks for *qualitative* observations are not quite so 'cut and dried'. While these depend largely on the observations required of you, it is possible to make the points by means of a few illustrations:

- 2 marks
  'The measurement and units are correct, but the drawing is poor.'
  'The observations are sometimes relevant, but tend to include terms like "big" which are meaningless unless used in comparison to another object.'
- 4 marks
  'The measurement and units are correct.'
  'The drawing is inaccurate in several details, nor has it been drawn twice the size (as requested).'
  'The table is clear and well laid out, but not all differences are mentioned.'
- 6 marks
  'The measurement and scale of the drawing are good.'
  'The table is well laid out and the observations include nearly all the relevant ones.'
  'The student has included particular features about the material which will ensure the top mark.'

4.4 Coursework requiring these skills

Both observation and measurement are so central to the nature of science that the opportunities for assessment of these areas are unlimited. Most of the qualitative observations tend to involve biological material, while the true measurement is more frequently allowed in physics or chemistry. Most of the examples of coursework in Chapter 4 involve observation and measurement.

SUMMARY

1. Keep 'the question' in mind.
2. Relevant observations answer the question.
3. Neatness matters.
4. Accuracy matters.
5. Look, think, then record.
6. Drawing rules will help.

UNIT 5 RECORDING AND COMMUNICATION

Whenever something is communicated well, the **intended** message is received quickly and without any confusion. Science has relied on good communication throughout its history. At GCSE level, *recording* forms the link between observations and conclusions. It is therefore vital that recording is as clear as possible. If there is any confusion about what you actually measured or saw, then it is impossible to reach logical conclusions.

During assessment activities recording is doubly important as it gives the written *evidence* of what you have achieved.

Do not get the impression that a well recorded set of results will always fit an exact pattern. In fact the nature of experimental work is such that this happens very rarely. **It is vital that you record what you actually see**. This is one occasion when you should *not* try to predict the result before taking readings. Many assessment schemes ask you to suggest improvements to the method as part of the summary. It is this time that you can discuss what you would have *expected*, and can suggest reasons why your experiment gave different results. Indeed the greatest credit often goes to those who can **logically** suggest explanations for any strange results. At times you may be tempted to just ignore a particular result because it is different from all the others. What to do about 'exceptions' will be made clear in the next unit, but for the moment keep it in mind that *all* results should be recorded.

5.1 The 'formal' write-up

In some experiments you will be asked to record more than just the results. At times you may be asked to do a much more formal 'write-up'. There is a standard system which satisfies most assessment schemes. You may find that reading Chapter 3 will be very useful for such formal write-ups, as well as for organising your own investigations!

Write up your experiments in properly separated sections. These are most often labelled:

- **Aim**
- **Hypothesis**
- **Apparatus**
- **Method**
- **Results**
- **Conclusions/Discussion**

It is important from the point of view of your own 'mental organisation' that you are sure what each of these stands for, and that you do not mix them up.

AIM

The point of the experiment, often expressed as a question.

HYPOTHESIS

The hypothesis is an idea or assumption. It often takes the form of an 'educated guess' which is based on observations. In an experiment or investigation a hypothesis can be *tested* by making new observations which relate to it. In your conclusion or discussion you will either accept or reject your original hypothesis. If you reject it, a modified version may be suggested to help explain **all** your observations. Or maybe you will have to re-think it completely! See Chapter 3, Unit 3 for details.

APPARATUS

Here you might list the apparatus used, or perhaps draw one or more diagrams, which should follow the drawing rules mentioned in the last section.

METHOD

This is an organised list which states exactly **what you did**. The method does not refer to the results in any way. Note that the term 'list' has been used. The best way to write your method is to list, point by point, what you did during the experiment (or plan to do, if it is possible to plan that far ahead!). A well-written method would allow someone who knew **nothing** about the experiment to repeat **exactly** what you did.

RESULTS

An organised record of **what you saw, observed or measured**. The result should not have the word **because** in it. As soon as you start looking for *reasons* why certain things happened, you are no longer the observer, but have started to *interpret* your findings. This should be left until all your observations are complete. The only exception to this rule occurs when you are recording results in a table in which the last column is called 'inference' or 'conclusion' ('flame tests' and 'food tests' could fit into this category).

CONCLUSIONS

This is fully described in the next unit, but for the moment let's call it a summary of any patterns/laws/rules which the results show you. Don't worry if occasionally it's a summary of what you didn't find! You should refer to your aim and/or your hypothesis (if you included one). Always look very hard at your results, or graph, or chart, and think carefully before you write anything down at all. Make sure that what you *do* write is a reasonable, or valid, deduction based on **your** results. What you write must make sense to you and to anyone else who reads your work!

DISCUSSION

In the work of 'real' scientists this is probably the most important part of a report! A discussion may form part of your conclusion, or you may feel it necessary to add a separate section. It is in this section that you should 'evaluate' what you have found from the whole experiment or investigation. You might consider things like:

"Useful things to consider in your evaluation of the experiment or investigation."

- Were there any human errors in my experiment/investigation?
- Did I manage to control all the variables (Chapter 3, Unit 4.1) that had to be kept constant?
- Were some variables impossible to control?
- What more could I have done to control or avoid these?
- Did the quality/functioning of my apparatus/equipment affect the results?
- What improvements could be made?
- Are there any further investigations or experiments that could be done?
- Is there any 'science theory' work I have done that is relevant?
- Do my results and conclusions match the known 'facts'?
- Was the investigation or experiment a success?
- What could I have done if I had more time and equipment?

Evaluation

Evaluation is extremely important in science. Questions like the ones above will show your teacher (examiner) whether or not you have understood the purpose of the experiment and how it relates to the background theory. You will find that some of the practical assignments are much more 'open-ended' than others and leave you free to devise your approach with as much originality as you can. However, other assignments will expect you to follow very precise details on how to proceed, what to measure and how to record results.

Always follow your teacher's, lecturer's or examiner's instructions in every detail. Most marks are lost by students who did what they **thought** they had been asked to do, instead of what was really asked!

5.2 How much detail?

When considering *which* things to include in an account of an experiment, it is worth keeping in mind the points made in Unit 4 about *relevance*. If you noticed a certain detail and feel it to be relevant, then record it. Here are some points about the various parts of an experimental account that you will need to apply in your practical work in order to be successful:

METHOD

- Use the 'list' method.
- Always give the *amounts* of chemicals used, and include the *units*.

RESULTS

- Where possible use a table to record results.
- Do not give too much accuracy.
- If you are taking a number of readings and then giving an *average*, make sure your table shows this.
- If you are using a table for an experiment that gives a colour change, do not put a tick or 'positive' in the column marked 'colour change'. Record in the column what you saw.

GRAPHS

Graphs are a specialised form of communication. You can easily get full marks for a graph if you follow a few guidelines:

1 The **dependent** variable (Chapter 3, Unit 4.1) goes on the **vertical** axis, and the 'uncontrolled' or **independent** variable on the **horizontal** axis. Time almost always goes on the horizontal axis. If, however, you are measuring how fast something happens in order to calculate a *rate*, then the time taken would be on the vertical axis.

2 Very few experiments lead to 'perfect' straight-line graphs. Nevertheless most will show a pattern. If the pattern is definite enough, then draw a 'line of best fit'.

3 **Not all graphs start at the '0-0' point (origin).** If you are measuring the rate of a reaction at different temperatures, and your range of temperatures is from 10°C to 90°C, then your graph could look like the one shown in Fig 2.7. You do not have any reason for joining the 10°C point to the origin. If you do, you are saying that the reaction stops at 0°C. This may be possible for some (especially biological) reactions, but your results do not show that it happens, so you cannot include it.

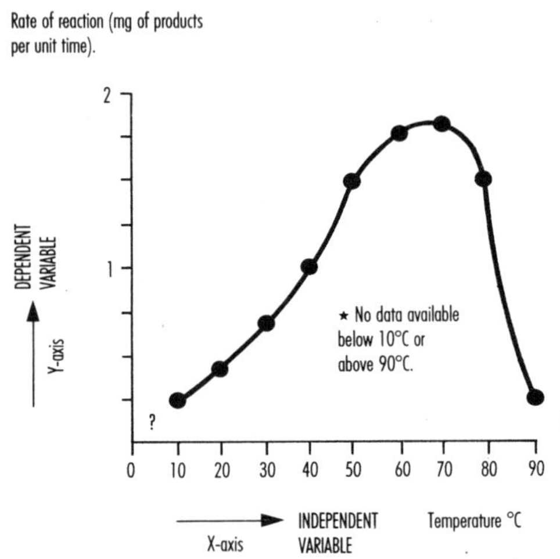

Fig 2.7
Rate of reaction at different temperatures

PREFIXES AND UNITS

The units used in science are as important as the actual measurements. The agreed units are as listed and each may be prefixed to form sub- or multiple units:

Sub-multiple	Prefix	Symbol
10^{-2}	centi	c
10^{-3}	milli	m
10^{-6}	micro	μ (Greek letter-mu)
10^{-9}	nano	n
10^{-12}	pico	p
Multiple	**Prefix**	**Symbol**
10^{3}	kilo	k
10^{6}	mega	M

Quantity	Unit	Abbreviation or Symbol
1 Base units		
length	metre	m
mass	kilogram	kg
time	second	s
electric current	ampere	A
temperature	kelvin	K
2 Derived units		
time	minute	min
frequency	hertz	Hz
force	newton	N
energy	joule	J
heat	joule	J
work	joule	J
pressure	pascal	Pa
power	watt	W
electrical potential difference	volt	V
electromotive force	volt	V
electric resistance	ohm	Ω (Greek letter-omega)
electrical capacitance	farad	F
3 Other units in common use		
volume	cubic metre	m^3
volume	litre	l
energy	kilowatt hour	kWh
temperature	degree Celsius	°C
temperature	degree Centigrade	°C

Many students choose to record their results 'in rough' before preparing a neat copy. Unless your writing in the laboratory as you work is totally unreadable, this is *not* a good idea. It will take longer and it gives another opportunity for mistakes.

5.3 How marks are awarded

- 2 marks – drawings show only the major features. Description is very general. Some units are wrong or missing. Graphs are incomplete or inaccurate.
- 4 marks – drawings show reasonable detail. Results tables used, but observations superficial. Graphs show at least one error.
- 6 marks – drawings are good in terms of scale, detail and labelling.
  Results recorded accurately and efficiently, with correct units. Graphs are perfect.

5.4 Coursework requiring these skills

- Effect of temperature on the action of yeast.
- Comparing two water samples for hardness.
- Investigation of taste.
- Heating crystals.
- Lots of examples are provided in Chapter 4.

SUMMARY

1. Efficient communication is as simple as possible, while giving enough detail.
2. Clarity is important.
3. Neatness.

UNIT 6 INTERPRETING INFORMATION

Some scientists would say that science starts when you have to *interpret* information, though many would give the skills of observation just as much importance. There is no doubt that *both* skills are necessary to a true scientist. In GCSE, however, the assessment on *interpreting information* may be the first time you have looked for cause *and* effect.

Within the idea of cause and effect lies the skill involved in interpreting information. When you can look at some experimental results and say that something happened *because* of something else, you have found the cause and the effect.

Suppose you are asked to heat some unidentified blue crystals and find out how they change as a result of heating. You have recorded that they lose mass and change colour to become white. You have also spotted some condensation on the neck of the test tube, which you have tested and found to be water. So far so good, in that you have *observed* and *recorded* everything you need in order to give an *interpretation*. Here are a number of possibilities. See what you think of these:

a) 'The crystals were burnt by the bunsen, and the heat formed the condensation.'

b) 'The crystals were copper sulphate and heating dried them out.'

c) 'The crystals contained some water which was driven off by the heat.'

d) 'The gases in the bunsen flame made the water, and the heat changed the colour of the crystals.'

Answer c) is the correct one, since all of the others have something in them which is **untrue**, or which **does not follow from the observations recorded**.

Answer a) is wrong because you cannot say the crystals were burnt, and heat does not form condensation.

Answer b) is wrong because you cannot be certain that the crystals were copper sulphate. You have not been given that information, and there might be other crystals that look just like copper sulphate.

Answer d) *assumes* that the bunsen gases form the water. If they did, then how did they get into the test tube?

If there is one error that occurs more than most, it is in stating **more** than the results support. The ability to recognise the copper sulphate in the example above is not worth anything, and naming it will actually cost marks.

The skill of *extracting* information is the skill of logic, and there is no doubt that some are better at it than others. However, it is a skill that can be learnt by attention to a few small details.

6.1 Extracting data

In its simplest form, this means looking at the results of an experiment and picking out the information you require in order to answer the question expressed in your 'aim'. In many experiments there will not be very much to it. Suppose you have separated the components of a soil sample by shaking it up with some water and then letting it settle out over a period of hours. It is then possible to record several things that will form your results. You can also draw your soil layers. The only further extractions possible are to count, measure and maybe identify those layers.

At a more complex level, interpreting data can involve graphs and charts.

In some assessment schemes there is an experiment in which you are asked to wire up a light bulb, as in Figure 2.8a). You then have to measure the potential difference (voltage) across it, with different currents going through. If you know your physics, you may recognise Ohm's Law (See Fig 2.8b). This law states that the voltage is **proportional** to the current. In other words, as the voltage increases, so does the current. However, having taken your results, you plot a graph as shown in Figure 2.8c). The graph agrees with your expectations, but only up to a point. As you can see, the readings with higher currents and potential differences do *not* lie on the expected straight line. If you hope to get full marks, then you should try to *interpret* this. What else could be happening that would affect the behaviour of the bulb? As the current and voltage increased the light from the bulb was brighter, so what was happening to the filament?

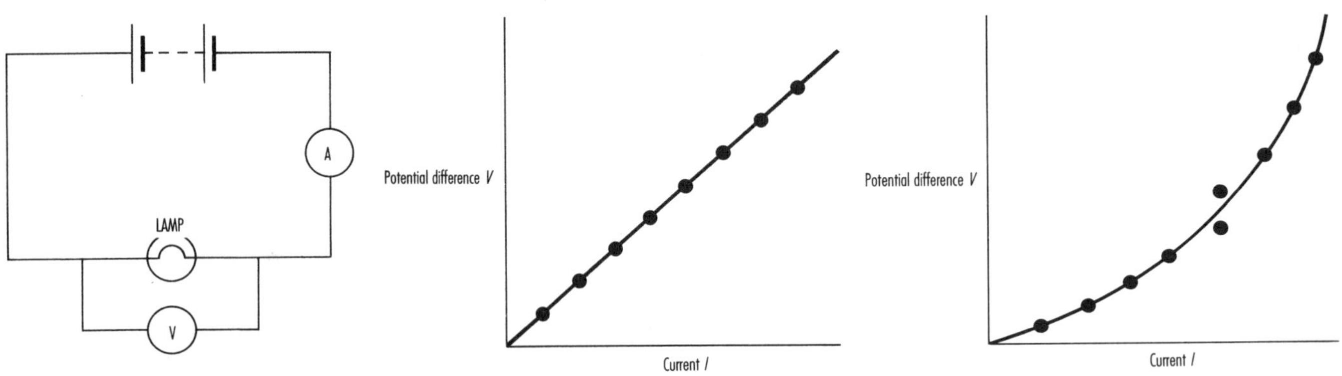

a)

b) Ohm's law

c)

REMEMBER: The gradient of this graph has a constant value, obtained by dividing the potential difference at any point by the current. The value of this constant gradient is known as the **resistance** R of the conductor. The unit of resistance is the **Ohm** (Ω).

$\frac{V}{I}$ = constant (R) (Ohm's law)

hence V = IR

DON'T FORGET: In a light bulb V/I is found to increase with temperature, that is R is not constant but increases as the temperature of the filament of the bulb increases.

Fig 2.8
Investigating Ohm's Law

Answer – It became hotter, thus affecting its **resistance** to the electric current.

The person who finds this interpretation has certainly used his or her brains. But even if they didn't know that temperature affects electrical resistance, could they have reached this answer? Let's look again at the graph. The last few points in Fig 2.8c) are all 'out of line', and they seem to be out by an increasing amount with each successive one. If time permits, the investigators will have repeated a couple of measurements to make sure their results were accurate. When they have confirmed their results, they leave themselves with two choices. They can either ignore the 'strange' results, *or* they can try to find a reason for them. In observing the light getting *brighter*, they only have a short way to go to reach the idea that the filament is getting *hotter*. Of course, if you *know* about resistance and temperature, it will all be much easier, but it is **not** impossible even if you do not!

"Try to give a reason for any exceptions you have found."

So, in the extraction of data you cannot afford to ignore the exceptions.

6.2 Processing data – calculations

There are many calculations involved in science. Those who are good at maths definitely have an advantage. However, even if you are someone who gets all the answers wrong, this still does not mean that you need to fail when assessed in this area. There are no assessments on which all of the credit goes to the good mathematicians. You are to be assessed on your **science**, not your maths. The marks for the science part of the assessment will far outweigh those for the final calculations. This does not of course mean that the calculations do not matter! While accepting that full marks probably involves getting the right answers, a *good approach* will get nearly all the marks and will also help you to get the right answers. A good approach means following these guidelines:

“Using this approach to your calculations you should ensure that you get marks for this skill.”

a) Write out each line of a calculation in full, making sure that it is clear where each number has ‘come from’.
b) You will usually be given the formulae you need to use. You still need to write them down at the start of any ‘sum’ that they are used in. Then the numbers can be substituted on the next line.
c) Most Exam Groups and teachers allow the use of calculators. If in doubt about this, ask! When you are using a calculator, try to keep an eye on the answers it gives as you use it. If you multiply 2.1 by 39.5, and get an answer of 829.5, then look closely. Your ‘sum’ is roughly the same as 2×40. In your head this quickly comes to 80, so you have hit the wrong button on the calculator. The correct answer is 82.95.
d) By knowing *common examples* you can sometimes spot mistakes. If you are calculating the density of various substances, some of which float on water, and you find the density of a ‘floater’ to be 8.2g cm^{-3}, then you have made a mistake somewhere. You know this since all things which float on water have a density of *less than* 1.00g cm^{-3} (the density of water).
e) You can work out *units* from your calculations as long as you write them into every line. Make a point of learning about the way units are written, so that cm s^{-1} (or $^{-2}$) make sense. Remember that any power or index with a minus sign (−) in front of it means that it is the thing you *divide by*, since it means ‘per’, as in cm per second (cm s^{-1}) or g per cm^3 (g cm^{-3}). Often an oblique line ‘/’, will be used to mean ‘per’. The units above would then be written as cm/s or cm/s^2 or g/cm^3. Be ready for *both* sorts if you can; ask your teacher if you need help.

6.3 Recognising patterns

A *pattern* on wallpaper is a shape or structure that is repeated. In science we are looking for repeatable changes, i.e. we are often looking to see how other things change when we change **one thing**. The idea of taking several results is so that there is more information on which to base your pattern. When looking for patterns you usually look at only **two** sets of observations and see how one set changes as you change the other set. One of the most important skills when it comes to designing your own experiments is making sure that there are limited **variables** (see Chapter 3). In most of the ‘teacher-directed’ assessments, that choice has already been made for you. The results you have to find are usually fairly clear (with the exception being the ‘open observation’ type of exercise), so pattern finding has been made that much easier.

There are some terms which are useful in describing patterns:

▶ **Proportional**

If A is proportional to B, then A increases by the same amount when B increases by the same amount. **Note** that they do not have to increase by the same amount *as each other.* For example:

A	*B*
1	5
2	10
3	15
4	20

In this case, A is *proportional* to B, even though B increases by 5 when A increases by 1 (see Fig 2.9).

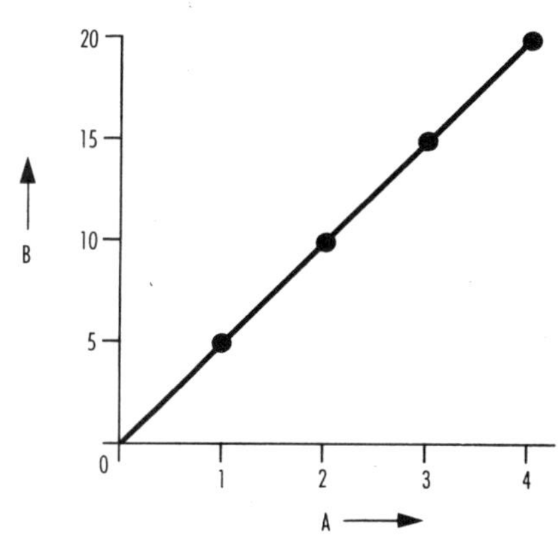

Fig 2.9
Proportional relationship graph

- **Inversely proportional**
  This is the relationship between two quantities whose *product* (times each other) is a *constant*. When two quantities are in inverse proportion, their graph is a *hyperbola* (see Fig 2.10).

A	*B*
2.0	7.5
1.0	15
0.5	30
0.25	60

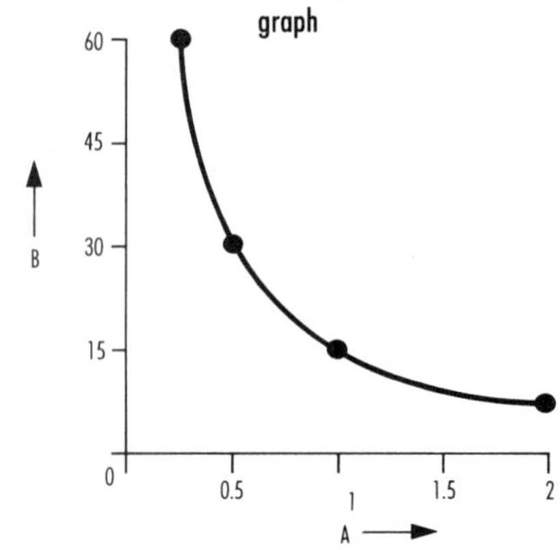

Fig 2.10
Inversely proportional relationship graph

In maths, these two possibilities could be written either as

$A = k \times B$ or $A = \frac{k}{B}$

Try to work out which one comes from which relationship. Find a value for k in each case.
Answer:

First relationship: (*Proportional*)	$A = \text{constant (k)} \times B$, $k = 0.2$
Second relationship: (*Inversely proportional*)	$A \times B = \text{constant (k)}$, $k = 15$

If you use the term *proportional*, you must use it accurately. It has a very precise meaning, and the time to think about proportionality is when you have drawn a straight-line graph. It is also a good idea to avoid the term when doing biological experiments, since there are usually so many variables that claiming proportionality is very risky.

- **Depends on**
  This is a useful term to use in those cases where you are not sure if the evidence is conclusive. It is not as exact a term as proportional, and will suffice in many biological situations. You could say that the rate of an enzyme-catalysed reaction depends on temperature, but you would never say it was proportional to temperature.

6.4 Drawing conclusions

Many of the assessment exercises ask you to draw conclusions **based on your results.** The importance of **not** bringing in any other information you may know cannot be stated too strongly. Once again, there is a need for **logic**, and this need applies especially to your explanation of the conclusions made. Your conclusions should be clear and precise. You cannot afford to be vague. If you have trouble doing this, then try taking the events of the experiment one by one. Then, for each event, jot down one statement that uses the word **because**. After you have done that it will be easier to write out your conclusion.

At times you will not be able to write definite conclusions. This is often the case when your results are not as expected. If this should happen, don't be afraid of writing that you are unable to form any clear conclusion due to insufficient data. But back up such a statement with some reasons *why* the data is not complete. If the truth is that you have made a mess of taking the readings, then say so; but point out the fact that you would have repeated the experiment if you had been given extra time. Another useful point to make in these circumstances would relate to the *method* you have used. If you can suggest any future improvements to the method, you may be given credit for them. Remember that the accuracy of your measurements depends to a large extent on the instruments you have used.

6.5 How marks are awarded

- 2 marks – acceptable graphs are drawn only with considerable assistance. Descriptions of the effects of changes are simple and qualitative. (For example, in the light bulb example such a statement as 'the current increased as the voltage increased'.)
- 4 marks – reminders needed about the proper use of graph paper (labelling units and deciding on the appropriate axes). Conclusions clearly state any relationships shown and include reference to any anomalous results.
- 6 marks – graphs are perfectly produced without any assistance. Clear comment is made on any anomalous (strange) results, and the sources of experimental error are mentioned.

Conclusions will often be quantitative statements referring to the effect of one factor on another.

6.6 Coursework requiring these skills

Any exercise which includes questions like those below will be a measure of your ability to interpret data.

- 'What do the results show?'
- 'What are the sources of error in the investigation?'
- 'Which results do not fit a general pattern? Explain these.'
- 'What conclusions can you draw about . . . ?'
- 'Can you think of any (other) reason for the difference?'
- 'Write down the names of the substances in order of their ability to conduct heat.'

The examples in Chapter 4, Units 2, 6, 7, 8, 9, 10 and 11 illustrate the use and need for these skills.

SUMMARY

Your 'check-list' this time is in the form of questions to ask yourself after you have finished interpreting the data. You should be able to answer 'yes' to all of these questions:

1 Has the entire experiment made 'sense'?
2 Have I 'stuck to the point'?
3 Are my explanations clear enough for someone to follow, even if they did not know the experiment?
4 Did I explain **all** the results?
5 Have I concentrated on the important variables?

UNIT 7 FOLLOWING SAFE WORKING PROCEDURES

In nearly all experiments, this area of assessment involves the skills of **awareness**, **concentration** and **control**. These are personal qualities which some people show most of the time, but which others have difficulty with. One point to bear in mind is that the 'winners' in the whole area of coursework are giving themselves a 'start' when it comes to the dreaded examination 'results'. 20% or more of the marks can be yours *before* you have written a single word in the written examination papers, after which the task of getting the grade you need will be easier.

Quite apart from the exam requirements, working *safely* will mean that the range (and 'enjoyability') of experiments you can carry out will increase. Teachers will not risk complex and detailed work using expensive apparatus with groups who do not work safely. So if you enjoy your science, make it safe science!

7.1 Protection for people

Hopefully, by the time you reach GCSE, you will have a good awareness of the situations in Science which are 'dangerous'. However, there is one danger you probably have not thought about, which is by far the most dangerous to your own health and that of others. This 'danger' cannot be predicted, and only by facing the reality of human nature can it be avoided. The greatest danger in a laboratory is **you** and the other people in it. While you cannot protect others from their own actions, your thoughtful actions will make sure that **you** are not a danger to yourself or to anyone else.

Protection comes from a Latin word meaning 'front cover'. Safety screens, safety goggles, laboratory coats, aprons, rubber or plastic gloves, and test tube holders will all protect you, **provided you use them**!

Can you spot any danger?

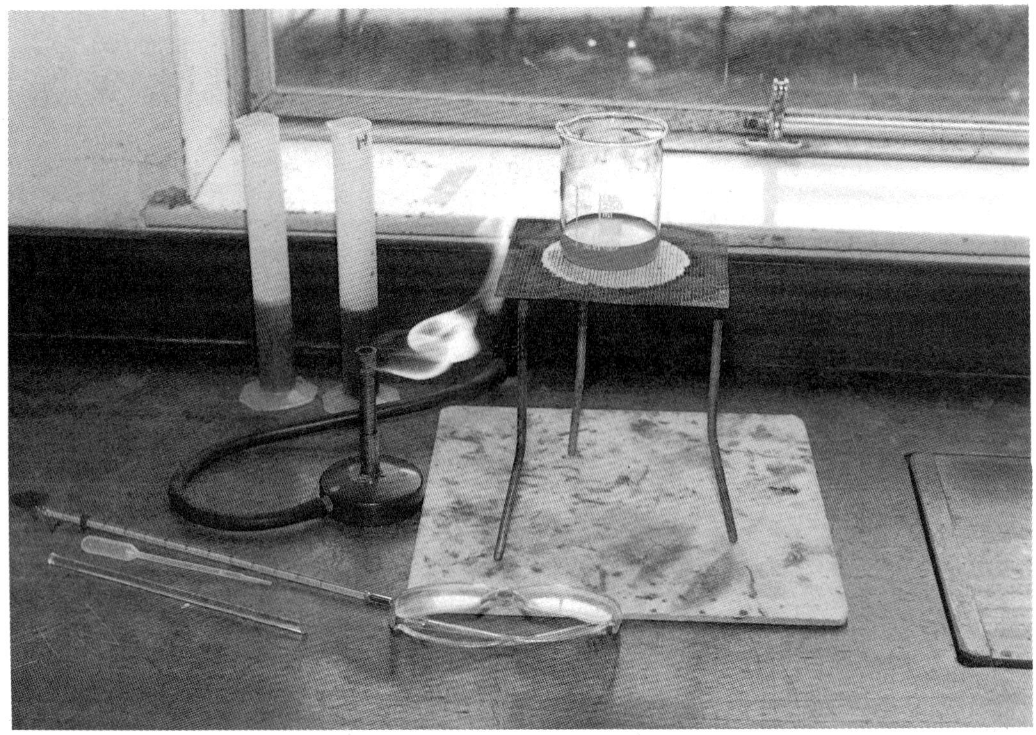

Obviously, there is a time for using each item on the list of dangerous chemicals in Fig 2.11. Experience, common sense and frequent reminders from your teachers will let you know when it is appropriate to use each item.

In every laboratory there should be a set of *safety rules*. Make sure you **know** and **apply** these rules. If you don't, then sooner or later an accident will result. If you are lucky no-one will be permanently disabled, but it's worth remembering just how dangerous some of the apparatus can be. The list in Figure 2.11 shows how some of the more dangerous chemicals could harm the **unprotected**.

Some chemicals have **hazard warning labels**. These will tell you just how dangerous each one is. Some examples are shown in Fig 2.12.

Fig 2.11
List of dangerous chemicals

name	state	dangers
acids	l/aq	corrosive; burns eyes and skin
alcohols	l	flammable, poisonous by mouth/skin absorption
alkalis	s/aq	caustic; attacks eyes and skin
ammonia	g/aq	attacks lungs; irritates eyes and skin
ammonium dichromate (VI)	s	causes ulcers and cancer; fire hazard
ammonium nitrate	s	irritates eyes and lungs; explosive
barium salts	aq	very poisonous by mouth/skin absorption
bleaching powder	s	corrosive, poisonous, explosive on heating
bromine	l/aq	corrosive, poisonous; liquid extremely dangerous
calcium (hydr)oxide	s	attacks eyes, lungs, skin, water violently
chlorine	g/aq	extremely poisonous; harms eyes and lungs
copper compounds	s/aq	very toxic; harm eyes, lungs, skin
Fehling's solution	aq	harmful to eyes and skin
hydrochloric acid	aq	burns eyes, lungs and skin
hydrocarbons	l/g	flammable; harmful to skin and lungs
hydrogen	g	flammable and very explosive with air
iodine	s/aq	burns skin; vapour attacks eyes and lungs
lead salts	aq	cumulative poisons by mouth/skin absorption
magnesium	s	fire risk; skin damaged by splinter heals slowly
mercury	l	cumulative poison by vapour inhalation
nitric acid	l/aq	harmful to eyes and skin; powerful oxidant
nitrates (nitrites)	s/aq	oxidants and poisons
phenolphthalein	s/aq	causes stomach upset and diarrhoea
silver nitrate	s/aq	corrosive; harmful to skin
sodalime	s	corrosive; attacks eyes and skin
sodium carbonate	s/aq	caustic to eyes and skin
sodium hydroxide	s/aq	very caustic and harmful to eyes and skin
sulphur dioxide	g	toxic; attacks lungs and causes bronchitis
sulphuric acid	l/aq	very corrosive; attacks skin and water violently
tetrachloromethane	l	causes cancer; vapour/skin absorption

Eye protection must be worn

Explosive
These substances may explode if ignited in air or exposed to heat. A sudden shock or friction may also start an explosion

Harmful
These chemicals are less of a health risk than toxic substances, but they must still be handled with care

Oxidizing
These substances may produce much heat as they react with other materials. They can create a fire risk

Corrosive
These chemicals destroy living tissue, including the eyes and skin

Highly flammable
These are solids, liquids or gases that may easily catch fire in a laboratory under normal conditions

Irritant
These substances are not corrosive but they cause reddening or blistering of the skin. The effect may be immediate or may only be seen after long or repeated contact with the chemical

Toxic
These substances are a serious risk to health and can cause death

Fig 2.12
Hazard warning labels

7.2 Avoiding accidents

If your reaction to the possibility of hurting yourself and others in the lab is a feeling of respect for safety, then you have made an important step towards becoming a **safe scientist**. The rules for safe working are all based on common sense, and you may have worked them out yourself by now. However, there is no harm in stating them again:

“Some important rules for safety.”

1 Always use the protective clothing/goggles/gloves provided.
2 Never *touch* chemicals.
3 Never *taste* or *eat* **anything** in the laboratory.
4 Never *inhale* chemicals.
5 Never point a ‘heating vessel’, e.g. a test tube, at anyone.
6 Think before you act – **be safety conscious.**

Since more than 90% of accidents in school science are caused by a failure to follow one or more of these rules, their value is obvious. It is the job of *every* scientist to apply rules like these. In industry a scientist who breaks such a rule and causes harm to someone else, could be held legally responsible.

IF AN ACCIDENT SHOULD HAPPEN

Thankfully most of the accidents that happen in school science are neither fatal nor disabling. However, they must be dealt with *correctly* and *quickly*. The first thing to do, even if no one is hurt, is to inform the teacher, who will have access to information about the required first aid. Even the simplest breakage of laboratory glassware should be reported. The mercury from a broken thermometer gives off very harmful vapour which must be dealt with in the correct way. Only when the situation is so serious that delay could make things worse should you act before reporting the accident to a teacher.

7.3 Disposing of chemicals

You will, without doubt, come across chemicals which need to be disposed of in a particular way. In this case the proper method will be stated by the teacher. Most of the chemicals you will use can be disposed of fairly easily by methods that involve either *dilution* with lots of water and disposal down the sink, or (in the case of solids) *collection* for later disposal or re-use. Do *not* put solids down the sink, even if they are in the form of grains, like sand.

7.4 GCSE marks for safety

There are very few (if any) exercises that are designed specifically to assess your ability to work safely. The Exam Groups that require this skill to be assessed include the assessment of safety in other experiments. So you have to work safely at the very time when you are concentrating on other aspects. Quite simply, you will have enough to think about without consciously having to think ‘safety’. The best way to cope with the need for safety is to make it a *habit*. By becoming used to working safely, you will reach a stage when it is second nature. Doing so will free your attention for the demands of the assessment.

"Working safely needs to become a habit."

It will be difficult to get your best possible score for observation while you are thinking 'Am I working safely?', so the time to consciously practise safe working is during your general laboratory sessions. This is when you have none of the pressures of an assessment. You can have a hard look at your work bench and ask yourself the following questions:

"Useful questions to ask yourself about your work bench."

- Does it look organised?
- Do all the bottles have stoppers on them?
- Are there any possibilities of test tubes or thermometers 'rolling'?
- Is the bunsen burner far enough away from flammable materials?
- Is the flame appropriate (safety, working, small or large)?
- Is the bunsen burner hose liable to knock anything over?
- Is any liquid away from the electric sockets?
- Have you labelled any samples of chemicals?
- Are your safety goggles over your eyes or, if you don't need them are they on the bench with the plastic lenses uppermost?
- Are there any spills of chemical solutions?
- Do you know where there is a cloth?
- Are there any books or papers where they may get wet if something does spill over?
- Is the floor in your area free from bags and other obstructions?

Hopefully you are able to answer 'yes' to most of these. However the list gives a few of the possible dangers, and only experience will help you to spot the others.

Having looked at your *surroundings*, the next thing to examine is your *mental attitude*. To work safely, an attitude of 'confident respect' is best. In other words an awareness, but not a fear, of the potential dangers.

The criteria used by the Exam Groups for marking safe working are as varied as the exercises they refer to. The reason for this is simply that safe working involves different things in different experiments and situations. You will find that safe working practices become part of your nature in time, and that you will not need to think about every safety precaution you should take. However, safety issues must always remain important for you in practical science. Careful consideration should be given to them *before* starting any practical session.

SUMMARY

1 Safety is your responsibility.
2 Protection and prevention are better than treatment with medicine.
3 Accidents don't just happen. They are caused!
4 Safety can be 'second nature'.
5 Safe science is successful science and can be fun too!

UNIT 8 WORKING WITH OTHERS

This skill is a particularly difficult one to assess, because gathering *evidence* of your ability to work with others is almost impossible. Those Examination Groups that do include this, tend to expect an 'impression mark' that is built up by one or more teachers over a two year period.

Co-operation and team-building skills do not come easily, but this is the way most scientists work. It is an important skill which is well worth working at. This skill is explored further in Chapter 3, Unit 1.2

Working effectively as a group, or a member of a group, is only one aspect of 'working together'. There are other people you need to consider: your teacher, other Science Department staff, the laboratory technicians, the resource technicians and the librarians. To get the best out of your coursework you will need to develop and to foster good working relationships with these people, all of whom can help improve the quality of your work.

Teamwork may include your teacher

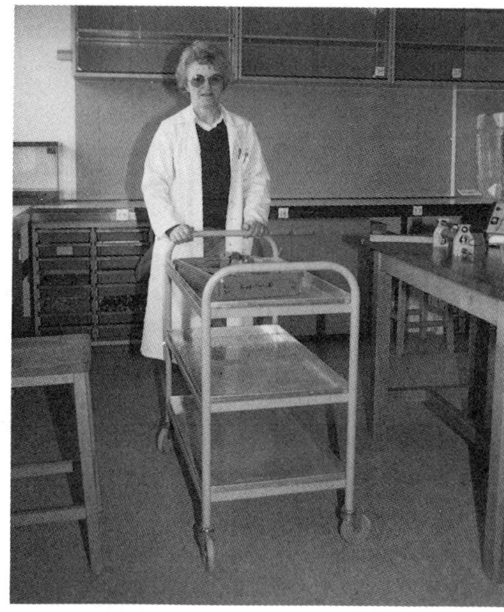

Technicians provide vital practical support for both staff and students

As a student, you will need to work WITH, rather than for your teacher. *Teachers* are your allies; they want you to do well and, within reason, will generally give you all the support you need. Remember they are busy people who have many students to support; some may actually teach hundreds of students each week. Be patient, but persistent – choose your time to approach the teacher or lecturer carefully. Be prepared to stay on for a few moments at the end of a lesson rather than to rush off with your friends. Teachers respond well to the 'flattery' of a student who stays behind to clear up a problem, or to explore an idea just a little bit further. Be concise though; teachers move according to the timetable, just like you, and have to fit in a cup of coffee, or a snack at lunchtime.

After your teacher, the *laboratory technicians* probably rank second. In some types of work their support can be very valuable. If your course involves assignments or projects they will be able to enhance your practical capability tremendously. Perhaps your school or college is involved in TVEI; if so, you will certainly have considerable responsibility for organising some of your own practical coursework.

To ensure the level of technical assistance and support you need it would be wise to:

- Treat technicians with consideration, be polite, show you are aware of how demanding and frustrating their work is.
- Remember that they are not well paid and often work overtime for no extra money.
- Be aware that they can often work miracles, if you give them good warning of your needs.
- Show them that you respect materials, equipment and property.
- Do your own cleaning-up and tidying – this is not their job, although they may have to waste time doing it.
- Ask their permission and advice when appropriate - many are well qualified and will be very supportive if given an opportunity to help.

There are probably many other points. But if you have now got an idea of what is meant by those listed, you might well get *enough* apparatus, *clean* apparatus, the *right* apparatus, etc. Technicians need a little 'psychological stroking', just like the rest of us! Show them that they are valued and you will get full value from them. Your teacher will thank you, because technical assistance is essential in modern science and happy laboratory technicians provide a better service than miserable ones!

The other people mentioned above also need to be treated with respect and courtesy if you are to get best value from them. The basic rule of 'treat others as you would wish to be treated yourself', is an excellent one to work by. Working *with* others brings much better results than working *against* them.

UNIT 9

CAN-DO TASKS

These tasks are often described as 'enabling tasks', because if you *can't* do them you probably won't make much progress in practical science. They appear in several GCSE schemes, and are an important aspect of the assessment in some (e.g. the Suffolk Co-ordinated Science course). They always take the form of simple practical skills essential to the work of scientists. Many of them sound quite simple and unimportant, but each has its place. Together they ensure safe, effective and successful science. Such 'can-do' tasks might include those in the following list:

- Can use a microscope.
- Can make a temporary slide (including use of stains and coverslip where appropriate).
- Can detect the presence of starch in a prepared solution or food.
- Can measure lung volume (vital capacity).
- Can use a key to identify living organisms.
- Can choose and use a Newton meter to measure a force (to the nearest scale division).
- Can identify both load and effort for any given machine.
- Can correctly set up a series circuit (with four components) from a circuit diagram.
- Can operate a power supply to light a lamp (e.g. select appropriate voltage, connect, make safety check).
- Can use a thermometer to measure the temperature of a liquid
- Can collect a sample of gas.
- Can measure a time interval to an appropriate degree of accuracy.
- Can retrieve information from a computer database.
- Can make a three-dimensional model from a pictorial representation.

“Practical skills essential to the work of a scientist.”

You will have noticed that even in the short list above there are some quite challenging activities. How many of your fellow students have problems when using a microscope, or setting up an electrical circuit? Obviously we all have to be *taught* how to do these things at some stage. It is your teacher's job to set up situations in which YOU will *learn* how to do these things. It is your job to make good use of the opportunities made available during science lessons, because it is often very difficult to learn these things from books. Practical experience is often a vital part of becoming a *can-do* person!

Usually these tasks crop up naturally during the work that you are doing; they are rarely special skill testing lessons. If your course involves this kind of assessment it is important that you are co-operative and helpful to your teacher, who will often have many students to assess. Get to know your teacher, make sure that you are 'seen' and, if you are able, help make sure that others in your class are not missed out. The better the 'working relationship' you can develop with your teacher and your fellow students, the greater the chance of success for everyone concerned. Always seek advice if you are uncertain about what you are trying to achieve – your teacher will be keen to see you achieve your best.

Let us look at a few examples of can-do tasks in a little more detail. You will find that even the simplest practical task can seem very complicated when written down, so there is no real substitute for learning by doing. Take every opportunity to get 'hands-on' experience, and if possible make your own records of correct procedures.

EXAMPLE 1 – CAN USE A MICROSCOPE

This is one of the first can-do tasks in the Suffolk Course, but most GCSE Examining Groups expect students to have developed this skill.

First, remember the microscope is expensive and very fragile, so don't be surprised if your teacher is a little nervous the first time your group uses those reserved for GCSE candidates. Treat it with *great care* and you will at least have your teacher on your side when it comes to assessment! Here are some simple essential rules to remember if you are to be a can-do:

- When transporting the microscope lift it by the *body* and put your other hand under the base.
- Place it on a level surface in a good even light.
- Check the working of the *focusing knob* – turn it just a small amount and notice what moves.
- Turn the *turret* so that the lowest power *objective lens* is directly below the *ocular tube*. This will always be the shortest one. In Fig 2.13 it is marked with the power × 5.
- Either stand or sit behind the *body* of the microscope so that you can look down it comfortably (avoid tilting it if possible, even if you think it looks more 'professional'!).
- Look through the *eyepiece* and move the *mirror* around until you can see a bright, even light (*never* direct sunlight!). If it is too bright, turn the *rotating disc* until a smaller hole is under the *ocular tube*; if too dark, turn to a larger hole.

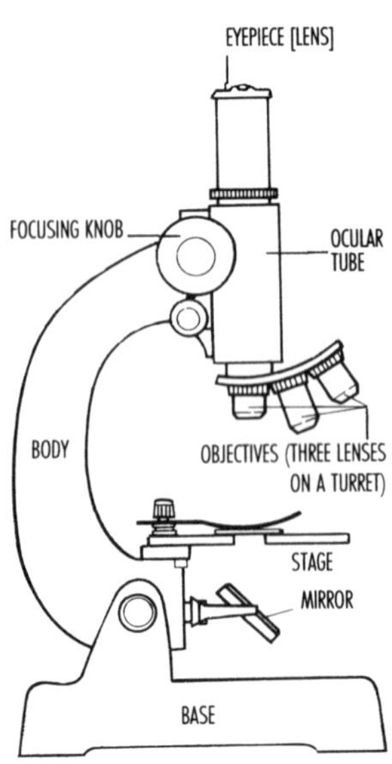

Fig 2.13
Typical compound microscope

- Put your *microscope slide* onto the stage, making sure it is clipped in place with the object you are to look at directly below the lens.
- *Not the obvious!* Look from the *side* of the microscope and use the *focusing knob* to bring the *objective lens* and the *stage* close together.
- *Now the obvious!* Look down the *eyepiece* and turn the focusing knob *very slowly towards you*, until the object you are looking at is sharp and clear. *ALWAYS REMEMBER – never look down the microscope and turn the focusing knob away from you at the same time!* If you do you risk shattering the slide with the objective lens. On some microscopes this is impossible, but it's best never to find out which!
- Once you have viewed the object on low power, if you need greater magnification turn to a higher-power objective lens and repeat the above. Often on good microscopes the objective lenses will be isofocal and very little adjustment will be needed.

To work out the magnification is very simple:
EYEPIECE POWER × OBJECTIVE POWER = MAGNIFICATION.
For example:
$10 \times 20 = 200$.

Microscopes vary a great deal, and you may find that even in your laboratory there are several types; certainly there will be a variety in your school or college. If the one you are using is unfamiliar, ask your teacher to demonstrate its operation for you.

EXAMPLE 2 – CAN MAKE A TEMPORARY SLIDE (INCLUDING THE USE OF STAINS AND A COVERSLIP WHERE APPROPRIATE)

Having acquired the skills needed to use a microscope, students usually progress to preparing their own temporary (rather than permanent) slides to view. Onion leaf cells are often the first specimens to be wet mounted. The cells are peeled carefully from a leaf in the onion bulb and placed in a drop of water on the glass slide. A very thin square of glass, the cover slip, is then gently lowered on top. To avoid trapping air bubbles, which most beginners usually find far more fascinating than the specimen, one edge is lowered first as shown in Fig 2.14. A good mount has no bubbles and is not flooded with excess water. Any water or liquid on the slide must be removed *before* it is placed on the stage of the microscope. The completed temporary mount should be flat and thin enough for light to pass through; it is a very common mistake to use specimens that are far too large.

To make features more obvious, stains are often used; the specimen may be mounted in the stain or the stain can be added after the first viewing by irrigation. Iodine (potassium iodide) is the usual stain for use with onion leaf cells. This technique is shown in Fig 2.15, and can also be used to introduce different concentrations of sugar or salt solutions in order to investigate the effects of osmosis at a cellular level.

Fig 2.14
Preparing a temporary slide

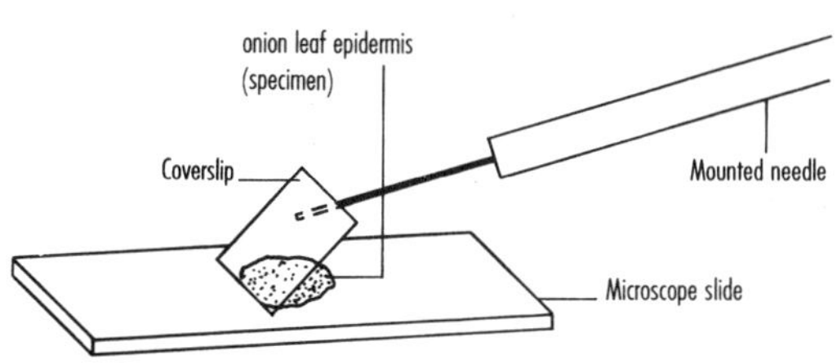

Fig 2.15
Staining by irrigation

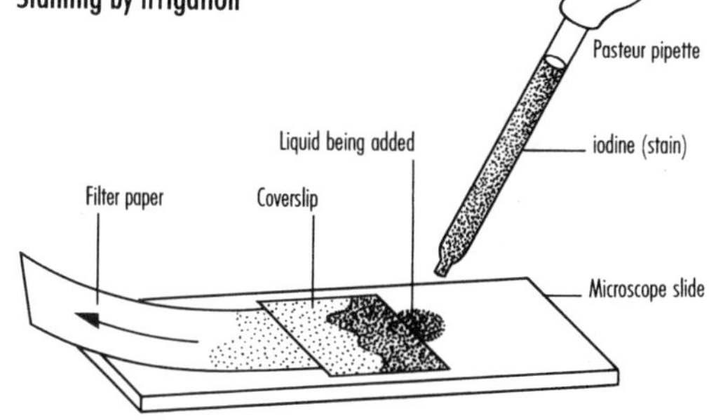

Other methods of mounting specimens are less common at GCSE level, but you may try *smears* and *squashes*. You will always be given full instructions when carrying out such practical exercises, so make sure you listen for all the 'tips' before you try for yourself. Permanent mounts are almost never attempted because of the time it takes to do the job properly. If your school or college has a collection of prepared permanent slides it will probably be worth a great deal of money. Take care if you are privileged to work with some of these slides. Their value will range from a few pounds to many pounds each!

EXAMPLE 3 – CAN USE A THERMOMETER (TO MEASURE TEMPERATURE OF A LIQUID)

There are many types of thermometer in common use today – alcohol in glass, mercury in glass and electronic thermometers are the ones that you might use in school or college. The mercury in glass thermometers are the commonest; they are quite expensive and very fragile. If you heat them even slightly above their range, or simply let them roll from a bench to the floor, the thin glass bulb containing most of the mercury is sure to break. If lots of thermometers are in use around the laboratory, your teacher will be very concerned for their 'safety'. He or she will have to face the laboratory technician at the end of the lesson to explain the losses, not a pleasant task! Expect no mercy if you break a thermometer – *you will have been warned!* It is also vital that you remember that thermometers only have one use – they are used to measure temperature. Don't be tempted to use them to stir either liquids or mixtures – stirring is a sure way to shatter the bulb!

When thermometers are manufactured they are calibrated to read temperatures under certain fixed conditions. Some require *total immersion,* and with these you must make sure that the whole of the mercury column is below the surface of the liquid whose temperature you are measuring. Many do not require total immersion and the depth of immersion necessary will be engraved or printed on the back of the thermometer. A 60 mm immersion is common, so beware: errors will occur (though very slight) if you do not use the instrument correctly. For most practical work such small errors are unimportant. GCSE boards do not usually require accuracy beyond about 1 degree Celsius, but if *you* are designing an investigation even small errors may be important to you.

Here are some simple essential rules to remember if you are to be a can-do:

- When transporting the thermometer, hold it carefully but firmly. Take great care when removing it from its plastic case. Place it away from edges and make sure it cannot roll (often a plastic roll-preventer is attached, forming one end of the case: *do not remove it*).
- Check that the thermometer covers the temperature range you require.
- Make sure that the thread of mercury has no gaps in it; it must be unbroken.
- Lower the bulb carefully into the liquid under test.
- Stir or shake the liquid before testing the temperature.
- Hold the bulb in the 'body' of the liquid, away from the sides and bottom of the container.
- Place your eye-level with the top of the mercury thread.
- Only record the reading when the mercury thread has stopped moving.
- The thermometer must be *in* the liquid throughout the time it takes you to record the temperature. Don't lift it out and up to your eye! *(You can do this with a medical thermometer, but that has been specially designed to be read after removal from the patient's mouth. Medical thermometers, and some others, are designed so that the stem acts as a magnifying glass to help you see the fine mercury thread. These are tricky to use until you are familiar with them.)*
- Take the thermometer out of the liquid after taking the reading and place it somewhere safe.

If you have any problems or break a thermometer consult your teacher. Mercury is an excellent liquid for use in thermometers, but should not be loose in the laboratory! So, again, a simple can-do seems very complex when written – learn the skill by doing, it's a lot less bother!

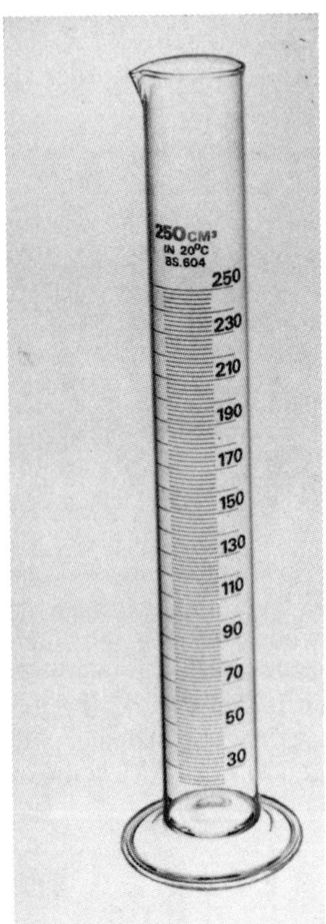

Fig 2.16
Glass/plastic measuring cylinder

EXAMPLE 4 – CAN MEASURE VOLUME OF A LIQUID ACCURATELY USING A MEASURING CYLINDER

Measuring cylinders are common pieces of apparatus which come in a variety of sizes and materials. They are used to measure liquid volumes from just a few cubic centimetres right up to about two cubic decimetres. Sadly they are not very stable and easily topple over. This tendency to fall over combined with their high cost can be a problem; the cheapest will cost at least £1, and large ones can cost as much as £20. Glass measuring cylinders are rarely intended for very hot liquids and can crack if subjected to rapid warming.

With all this in mind the manufacturers now produce them in a variety of plastics, as well as in combinations of glass and plastic like the one shown in Fig 2.16. The bases on the glass ones are traditionally circular and so these roll very well! Sometimes a hexagonal plastic sponge protector is fitted near the top to stop them rolling and this can stop them shattering when they topple over onto the work-surface. The plastic cylinders are much stronger but tend to be less accurate and are easily stained.

Here are some simple but essential rules to remember if you are to be a can-do:

- Wash out the cylinder with a little of the liquid you wish to measure.
- Carefully place it on a level surface.
- Pour the liquid into the cylinder slowly, avoiding spills.
- Check the volume, making sure that your eye is on a level with the meniscus (the bottom of the meniscus indicates the liquid volume contained in the cylinder).
- If necessary use a teat pipette to adjust the level to precisely the volume required (one drop from a teat pipette has a volume of about 0.05ml).

You can use the measuring cylinder in another way, to deliver *approximate* volumes of a liquid. If you fill it as described above, noting the volume contained, and then pour out (or use a teat pipette) liquid until the meniscus has gone down by the amount of liquid you require, you can deliver several small volumes of liquid quite quickly and accurately. If great accuracy is essential, then *graduated pipettes* or *burettes* must be used.

EXAMPLE 5 – CAN SET UP A SERIES CIRCUIT (WITH FOUR COMPONENTS) FROM A CIRCUIT DIAGRAM

An easy can-do for your teacher to assess, because your circuit will probably do something if it is correct. Lamps may light or a bell may ring. Some knowledge might be useful here – just what is a *series circuit*? Of course, it's a circuit in which the electricity has 'no choice' as to which path to follow, i.e. there are no branches in the circuit.

The circuit symbols used as a kind of shorthand in science are important as well. Make sure that you have a worksheet handy which helps identify the components in the circuit diagram. There are two slightly different series circuits shown in Fig 2.17; your can-do exercise might involve building such simple circuits exactly as shown in the 'standard form' diagrams. Can you find the lamps, switches, resistor and cells in these circuits? Usually such simple tasks form part of a practical session in which you will be investigating how different circuits and components behave. If you are working in a group make sure you build at least one circuit so that you can be seen to DO!

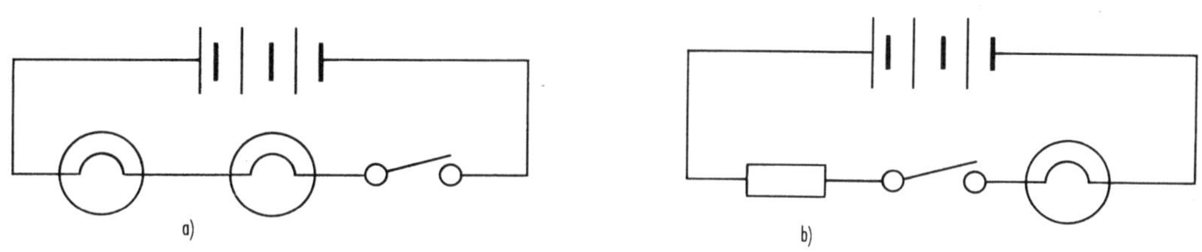

Fig 2.17
Series circuits with four components

EXAMPLE 6 – CAN TAKE A PAIR OF RELATED MEASUREMENTS ACCURATELY (SUCH AS DISTANCE AND TIME IN MEASURING SPEED)

Measuring speed is quite good fun if you make it so. The *ticker-timer* (Fig 2.18) used in your science lessons can easily be attached to a bicycle with interesting results, and checking the speed of cars on a main road can reveal a lot about drivers!

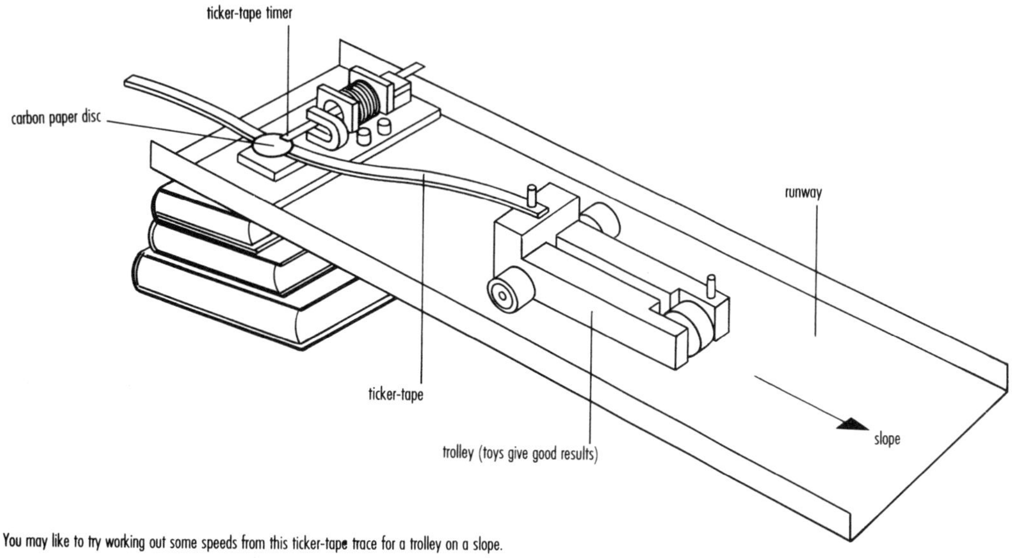

You may like to try working out some speeds from this ticker-tape trace for a trolley on a slope.

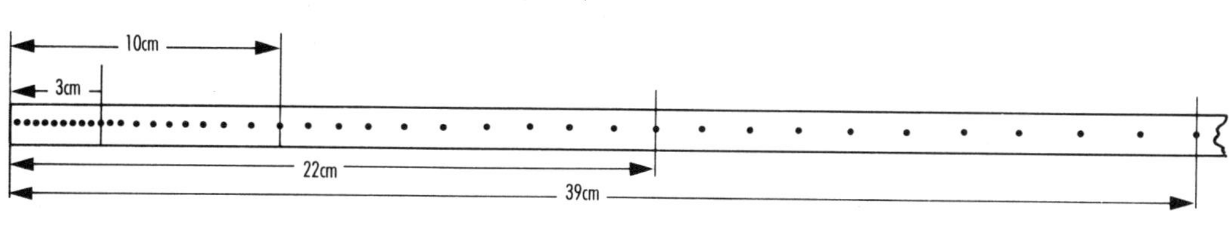

Fig 2.18
Ticker-timer and typical trace

The average speed can be calculated by measuring the time taken for an object to cover a measured distance:

$$\text{AVERAGE SPEED} = \frac{\text{DISTANCE}}{\text{TIME}}$$

A 'ticker-timer' and 'ticker-tape' can be used to measure speed over short distances and times. If you are to achieve this can-do, these suggestions will help:

- Connect the ticker-timer to a low voltage supply taking care to check what the timer requires (a.c. or d.c.), and its normal operating voltage.
- Set up your moving object, such as a trolley, on a slope as shown (Fig 2.18) and attach the ticker tape to the trolley, feeding it carefully through the timer.
- Switch on the timer so that it is ready to mark the tape with a dot 50 times a second.
- Check there is enough tape and that it is free to run through the timer.
- Release the trolley so that it pulls the tape through the timer as it runs down the slope.
- To find the average speed in the first fifth of a second carefully measure the distance covered by the first 10 spaces (one fifth of a second) in metres and use the formula given above:
  average speed = distance (m) ÷ 0.2(s)
- Your answer will be in metres per second.

If you have followed these guidelines you will have achieved another can-do. You will probably have noticed that the spaces between the dots increase, which means that the speed is increasing as the trolley rolls down the slope. This increasing speed is called *acceleration.*

It would not be difficult to fill a book with practical guidelines for can-do type tasks, but it would be rather boring to say the least! Rely on your teacher or lecturer to provide opportunities for you to learn these skills throughout your course. If you need advice about technique you should always ask. It is easier to *show* and explain, than to simply explain. Practise these skills and take a pride in the expertise you are developing in science. Mastery of these practical skills will increase your confidence and enjoyment of the subject.

CHAPTER 3

STUDENT-ORGANISED SCIENCE COURSEWORK

UNIT 1 STUDENT-DIRECTED PRACTICAL INVESTIGATIONS

This chapter reflects the extra responsibility that you may have been given for your learning in GCSE Science. Indeed there has been an overall increase in the importance of *student-centred* activity. All Examining Groups, in meeting the demands of the National Criteria, will assess your skills of planning, carrying out and evaluating investigations. At least one Exam Group goes even further, recognising that *teamwork* is involved in modern scientific research; for instance the Nuffield Co-ordinated Science Course requires that students be assessed on their ability to work with others.

As with the other skills, you will gain credit for student-organised practical work. However, you must take care not to let such experimental design and problem solving activities get out of hand. It is all too easy to spend too much time on such activities; you will have other priorities in your busy life and you should recognise them. Always strive to achieve a *balance* of effort within, and between, your GCSE subjects.

In your GCSE Science course you will be given opportunities to undertake work which shows the distinctive features of *investigation* in biology, chemistry and physics and, where appropriate, in other related sciences. You will probably notice that controlling variables and successfully repeating experiments which are mainly physical or chemical are a lot easier than doing similar biological investigations. Investigations involving living organisms tend to become quite complex very quickly. It is important to remember that the marks allocated for investigation skills only represent a very small percentage of the total mark for your GCSE Science. However, doing some 'real' science can be good fun as well as very rewarding for both you and your teacher.

If you are to be successful in working as a scientist you will need to develop fully all those skills dealt with in Chapter 2. Your teacher or lecturer will then attempt to prepare you for the challenge of your *own* scientific investigations. But many of the decisions will still be left to you. Your teacher will almost certainly scrutinise your plans *before* you start your experimental work in order to make sure that your procedures are safe, and that the materials and equipment you propose to use are available and appropriate.

Investigations may be completed during a single lesson, or over a series of lessons perhaps lasting for several weeks. If the latter is the case, you would probably be taking readings or measurements when 'convenient', i.e. while progressing with other aspects of your science course. This type of practical work gives your teacher a lot of flexibility. You may be assessed on any of the skills detailed in Chapter 2 while your investigation is under way. This may give you the chance to improve on your performance in past *teacher-organised* practical coursework assignments. Your teacher may also take this opportunity to generate *additional* assessments for you, for instance if you had been absent on an earlier occasion.

The problem being investigated might involve either familiar or new techniques. It could be a simple extension of ideas or be based on questions which have come up in class. Or the problem might be something entirely novel of your own choice. Often, very simple observations will provide a starting point for a suitable investigation. You may have been investigating the effect of exercise on the rate of heart beat, and a member of the group may have noticed that some students recover their 'normal' pulse rate faster than others. The question is 'Why?' There will be lots of suggestions, or hypotheses, as to why there are differences between individuals. Given the chance, you might now decide to investigate for yourself whether the length of the recovery period is related to the weight of the student, or to the student's resting pulse rate. Someone is bound to suggest that recovery time is a measure of 'fitness'! How is 'fitness' measured?

Now there are some useful starting points for many suitable investigations.

1.1 Working alone or with others

WORKING ON YOUR OWN

Working alone on an investigation is often easier than working with others. If your investigation is a simple one and you have thought it out carefully during the planning stage, it will have been approved by your teacher and there should be few problems. In this sort of assessment it is wise to ask for advice if you need it.

WORKING IN A GROUP

For many reasons this is usually the way almost all practical work is carried out in science classes. It is also the way in which most 'real' scientists work in research and industry. Teamwork is essential to the progress and application of science. If your course, like the Nuffield Co-ordinated Science Course, values and assesses this skill, you will need to make sure that you are really 'working' as part of the group.

If you are to score highly in this skill, you must have some 'key role' in the work of the group (Fig 3.1). Such key jobs might include:

"Roles you might adopt in group work."

- Safety Officer
- Equipment and Materials Manager
- Recorder of data, methods, etc.
- Report Writer or Presenter
- The Leader who liaises with the teacher

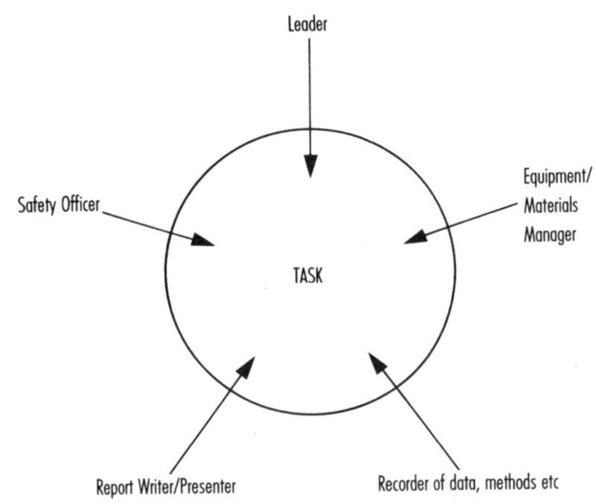

Fig 3.1
Your 'key role' in the group

In order to gain marks, your efforts within the group will be matched to written criteria (or descriptions) of performance, produced by the Exam Group whose course you are following. Your teacher or lecturer will be looking for things like the following, which are taken from the Nuffield course mentioned above:

- 2 marks – 'Is prepared to accept a limited role in the activities of a group but has only limited effectiveness in carrying it through'.
- 4 marks – 'Is willing to accept a limited role in the activities of the group and is effective in carrying out this role'.
- 6 marks – 'Is willing to accept a significant role in the activities of the group and is prepared to be responsible for seeing the role makes a contribution to the working of the group'.

This skill could be assessed either as an 'impression mark' built up by your teachers during your course, or by assessment based on one or two specific coursework assignments.

If the former is the case, your teachers will keep a record of their impressions of your activities during group work and this record may be required for moderation. Whichever method is used in your assessment, the messages are clear:

"Points to bear in mind in group work."

- Join in, don't sit back and watch.
- Find a job within the group.
- Do your job well.
- Try to vary the jobs you do in such assignments.
- Take a leading role at least once.
- Share and be considerate of others.
- If your group can't work together, be positive and get help from your teacher.

UNIT 2 PROBLEMS AND INVESTIGATIONS

2.1 Identifying the problem

In the early stages of an investigation, and particularly near the beginning of your course, you will usually get considerable help from your teacher. Exactly what happens may be determined by the Examining Group that is responsible for your course, so it is always a good idea to check an up-to-date syllabus. The likely starting point for any particular investigation will be a *topic*, or group of topics, chosen by your teacher. This choice will probably relate to work that you are currently doing in science.

When you get closer to the end of your course, and know a lot more about science, you may have an opportunity to exhibit this skill independently of current work. You can then use all the knowledge, skill and understanding you have gained. Your teacher or lecturer may present a problem for you, or you may have a chance to come up with your own problem to investigate. You might, of course, find that there is only choice from a limited list of options which are geared to the resources and equipment of your school or college. Don't be too disappointed, this activity can still be both challenging and rewarding.

Problems are usually generated when you *question* pieces of scientific information, or simply *observe* phenomena in the 'real' world. For example, you may read a statement in some advertising material for a new product:

RUSTOKIL
Rust prevention paint
No other anti-rust coating is more effective.

An interesting statement, and typical of an advertising claim. There could be several problems here, but the main one concerns the effect of *different* anti-rust coatings on the process of rusting. Rusting is a slow process, but are there ways of speeding it up? Would RUSTOKIL be best under all imaginable conditions? You can test this suggestion. There will, of course, be many practical problems to overcome if your investigation is to be successful.

Having *identified* a problem, try to keep your investigations *simple*. Always have a clear aim and know which questions you are trying to answer. The more *original* your investigation is, the better. Extra credit is often given to those who can identify a problem without help. It must, though, be realistic in terms of the availability of time and of cheap or easily-made equipment. The 'rusting' problem identified above will be referred to as our case-study example throughout this chapter.

2.2 Planning the investigation

Having settled your problem, *planning* the actual practical work is vital. Be realistic and keep your investigation simple. Most students make the error of devising over-ambitious plans at first, but a good teacher will soon offer more realistic advice. Only investigate *one* factor at a time. Don't allow yourself to be sidetracked into following up every fascinating 'red-herring' that you may come across.

Formal planning will help ensure that you follow a line of investigation that should produce results in the time available. It will also help you to avoid 'running out of steam' half-way through and, even more important, your being tempted to waste time by changing your mind once you have started.

AN OUTLINE PLAN

Your first plan does not have to be very detailed. It should define your area of interest, possible methods, apparatus and materials. This *outline plan* should be shared with others; perhaps other students, your parents if there is time, and certainly your teacher. In our rusting example, you could decide to paint 'iron' nails with a variety of anti-rust paints, then place them in a warm and moist atmosphere to encourage rusting.

PLAN A PILOT STUDY

This *pilot study* can be used to check that your intended methods are going to produce the desired results and that the materials and apparatus you have chosen are suitable. In our example, a treated and an untreated nail could be placed in a wet test tube in a warm place.

Keeping the nail wet and warm could present problems, as you would also need to ensure that oxygen from the air could get to the nails. The pilot study might help you come up with a detailed design.

CHOOSING APPARATUS

This may be important, as credit is usually given for the appropriate choice of apparatus. The pilot study should make this process simpler, but you may find that your teacher has already limited the choice for you. If you are given a free choice, you will probably be expected to produce a *list* of the apparatus you require. You will need to discuss this with your teacher and/or the laboratory technician. There are some sensible rules to follow:

- keep things simple if you can;
- use readily-available apparatus that you are familiar with;
- only include new apparatus or technology if you are sure you have the time to learn how to use them.

FORMULATING A HYPOTHESIS

If you are one of those fortunate students who knows *exactly* what to do, this can easily be your starting point. To form the idea, or *hypothesis*, which you are going to test by experiment, you do need a very clear idea of the background, processes and possible outcomes of your proposed investigation. The notion of 'hypothesis' is dealt with much more fully in Unit 3 of this chapter.

SYSTEMATIC LOGICAL PLANNING

Most Exam Groups award credit for the *systematic analysis* of a problem and for *logical planning*. It is possible to think about scientific problem solving as a *cycle* of events. Fig 3.2 illustrates just such a cycle. You may find this diagram useful in your planning.

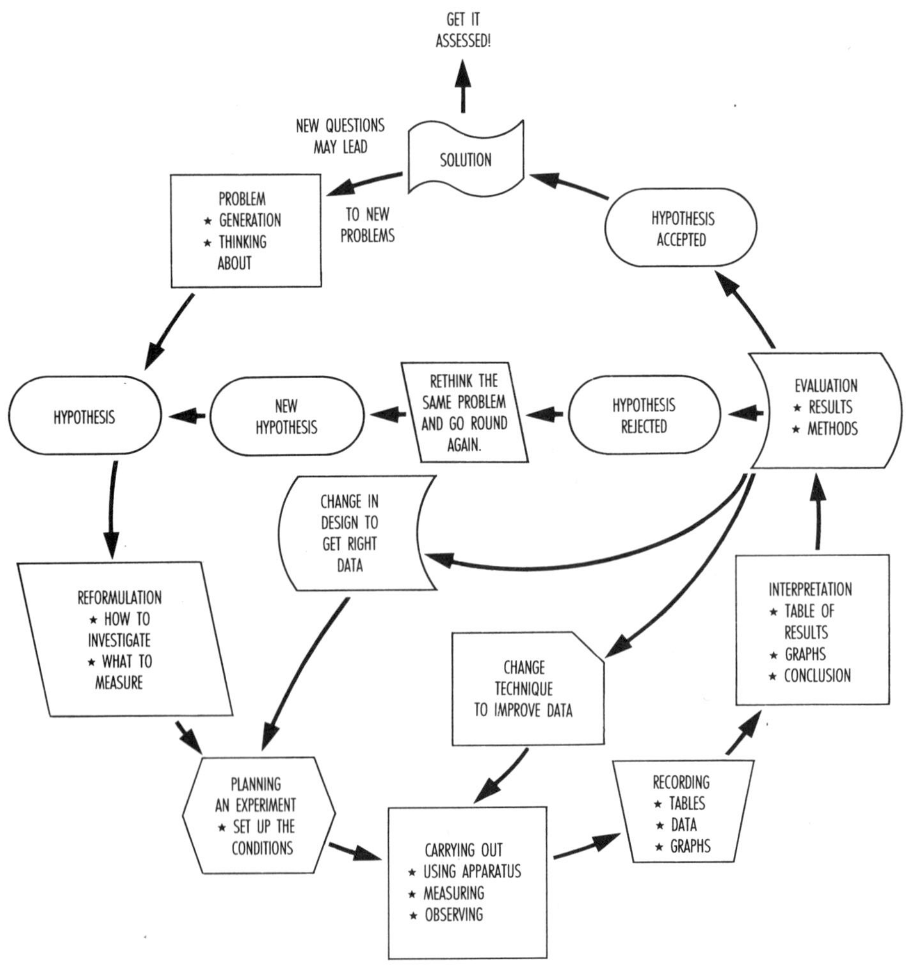

Fig 3.2
Systematic and logical planning: the problem-solving cycle

Presenting your investigation as a listed sequence of activities is a good way to show your ability. For example:

1 Obtain nails, select and clean required number.
2 Coat nails with chosen paints, using dipping technique.
3 Allow thorough drying of paints.
4 Clean test tubes, add $1cm^3$ distilled water to each.
5 Label tubes with paint names and control (unpainted).
6 Place nails in correct tubes.
7 Fit cotton wool bungs to tubes (reducing evaporation and allowing oxygen in).
8 Place tubes in warm cupboard.
9 Observe daily, recording onset and extent of rusting.

UNIT 3

FORMING AND TESTING A HYPOTHESIS

3.1 Forming a hypothesis

A *hypothesis* is an idea or assumption, and often takes the form of an 'educated guess' which is based on observations. In an investigation or experiment a hypothesis can be *tested* by making new observations which relate to it. If these further observations seem to *support* the hypothesis, then it has been 'confirmed' and it may be 'accepted'. If further observations fail to support the hypothesis, or even 'contradict' it, then the scientist must 'reject' it. Often, however, a hypothesis may only need 'modifying' in order to fit the new observations. A hypothesis which has been modified to fit all the observations may then be tested again; and so the process continues. In any real investigation there may be a whole succession of observations and hypotheses.

The stages in a scientific investigation are:

PROBLEM → HYPOTHESIS → EXPERIMENT → OBSERVATION → CONCLUSION

In the formation of your hypothesis you need to think 'imaginatively'. This is quite different to the critical and analytical approach you need to adopt when interpreting your experimental observations. In teacher-organised coursework sessions you may be given a problem and asked to devise a suitable hypothesis which can be tested. Or problems may simply appear during practical or fieldwork activities that you may be encouraged to hypothesise about.

Once you understand the idea you will find all sorts of opportunities to *practise* forming hypotheses. If your observation is that your science teacher is late for the lesson, possible hypotheses might include:

'Miss Jones is ill and will not attend the lesson today.'

'Miss Jones was out late last night and overslept this morning so missing this lesson.'

If, just as you have formed one of the above hypotheses, you see an RAC breakdown truck stop in the street outside the school and Miss Jones step quickly out, you may need to *modify* the hypothesis. We could continue the process, but Miss Jones would prefer us not to be nosey!

When you generate a hypothesis you should remember the following points:

"Useful points in generating a hypothesis."

- It should always make reasonable scientific sense.
- It should reflect available information and data.
- It should be simple.
- It should be testable, using techniques and resources which are available.
- It should be possible to 'accept it' or 'reject it' when tested.
- It should not be possible to 'half' accept or 'half' reject it.
- It need not be 'right'; it can be rejected, which is just as meaningful.

Using our RUSTOKIL example again, one hypothesis might be:

'RUSTOKIL paint provides better protection against rusting than any other paint tested.'

It is possible in the rusting experiment to make two sorts of observation. In the experiment described in Unit 2.1 of this chapter, **qualitative observations** were planned. These involved *recording* the onset, and extent, of rusting of each nail. Such results are **descriptive**.

Electronic balance – nail weighing

However the dry weight of *each* nail could also have been measured *each* day. This would have been a means of obtaining **quantitative observations**. These always involve **measurements**. Rusting is oxidation, or the gain of oxygen by the iron in the nail; so the greater the weight gain, the greater the rusting of that nail. A modern electronic balance would make the gathering of such data very accurate and quick.

Both qualitative and quantitative observations can be useful in scientific investigations. Suppose our experimental observations prove the hypothesis about RUSTOKIL paint to be true. Then, because painting on a substance is cheaper than some other forms of rust protection, such as zinc- or plastic-coating, it might be interesting to continue the investigation by comparing the performance of coatings *other than paint* with the RUSTOKIL. Another possibility might be to try harsher conditions, such as the effect of sea water on the performance of RUSTOKIL. In either case, new hypotheses would have to be formed and tested.

3.2 Testing a hypothesis

Testing a hypothesis will involve many of the skills and practical techniques detailed in Chapter 2. Once the experiment has been completed it will often be obvious whether the hypothesis should be accepted or rejected. Sometimes, however, the results will *not* provide such instant insight; in this case your careful *records* (Chapter 2, Unit 5) and thorough *interpretation* (Chapter 2, Unit 6) will provide the basis for any decision that is finally made.

If you are following the pattern of scientific investigation outlined at the start of this Unit, there can be no failure! You must be prepared to accept or reject your hypothesis, depending on your results. You are not 'wrong' if you have to reject it. The idea that it is 'failure' to have to reject a hypothesis is widespread; but this indicates a major misunderstanding of scientific investigation.

You need to be aware that there is the danger of getting the results you hope for, and missing those you *really* get. In making observations you must be meticulous, open-minded and honest. In many ways the scientist is like a child. If you see a thing, you must *say* that you see it, whether or not you thought you were going to see it. See first; think later, hypothesise, then test. But, always *see* first! Otherwise you will only discover what you were expecting.

UNIT 4 EXPERIMENTS AND 'CONTROLS'

4.1 Experimental design

There has always been a good deal of confusion in students' minds as to what an **experiment** actually is. Experiments are often confused with **exercises** and **investigations**. Each of these practical activities involves making scientific measurements and observations. However an *investigation* is different to the other two in that it may be short or long term. It may involve one, or a series of exercises or experiments. Exercises and experiments can be distinguished by the fact that the *experiments* always involve the comparison of *at least* two situations.

It is vital that you make sure that you have sorted out those differences, so that you do not join those students who waste valuable time designing *exercises*, when only experiments gain marks.

Sorting out experiments from exercises is not easy. To help you, some examples of simple exercises and related experiments are shown in Fig 3.3. The changing factors, conditions or situations that characterise experiments are termed **variables**. In any one experiment there should be no more than *two* such variables. All other factors, conditions or situations must remain constant (or as constant as is possible!) throughout the duration of the experiment.

There are two sorts of **experimental variable** in any experiment. The one changed by you, as the experimenter, is termed the **independent variable**; the one changed by the experiment is termed the **dependent variable**. Examples of both are shown in Fig 3.3.

Now that you understand what an experiment is, you will see that you can check your understanding by identifying whether the two sorts of variable are present in your plan. It is almost certain that the *independent* variable will be changed by you during the experiment, and it is probable that the dependent variable will change also in response to that change.

Exercise	Experiment	Experimental variables: Independent variable	Experimental variables: Dependent variable	Examples of fixed variables
determine the water content of blue copper sulphate	determine the water content of three different crystals, and compare them	different crystals	% water	mass of crystal used
finding your breathing rate at rest	finding how your breathing rate varies	different activites	breathing rate	same person same timer
measure the time for one swing of a pendulum	compare the time for one swing of pendulums of different length	length of pendulum	time for one swing	same mass same length same stopwatch
Does anhydrous copper sulphate get hot when you wet it?	Does anhydrous copper sulphate get hotter when you wet it more?	number of drops of water	temperature finally reached (max)	mass of copper sulphate same container
measure the extension of a spring for one known load	measure the extension of a spring for several known loads	the size of the load	extension of the spring	same spring same ruler same units

Fig 3.3
Distinguishing between exercises and experiments

Fig 3.4 is just part of a longer coursework investigation which led to the solution of an imaginary crime. The student's work that is shown was used, along with the rest of the investigation, to assess a number of skills. In this sample experiment the **time** is the

PRACTICAL COURSEWORK FOLLOW INSTRUCTIONS WITH CARE!

WHAT TO DO!

*Work in pairs! *You have the following per pair –
1 Thermometer **1** Cup (or similar) **1** Tea Bag **1** x 25 cm of milk
1 Stirring rod **1** Kettle (access at least!) **2** Printed sheets

***Both** members of each pair must complete a printed sheet!

METHOD SUMMARY –

Make a 'CUP' of tea using the equipment available. Measure its cooling using the thermometer. Record your results in a table in the space below. Plot your results on a graph on the squared section below. State exactly the time it took your tea to cool to 50 degrees Celsius in the space provided. TIDY ALL YOUR EQUIPMENT AWAY! Name and hand in the work!

NAME JOHN SMITH STG OGG 40

THE TABLE

Time	Temp
0 mins	85°C
3 mins	78°C
6 mins	74°C
9 mins	68°C
12 mins	64°C
15 mins	60°C
18 mins	54°C
21 mins	50°C

THE GRAPH

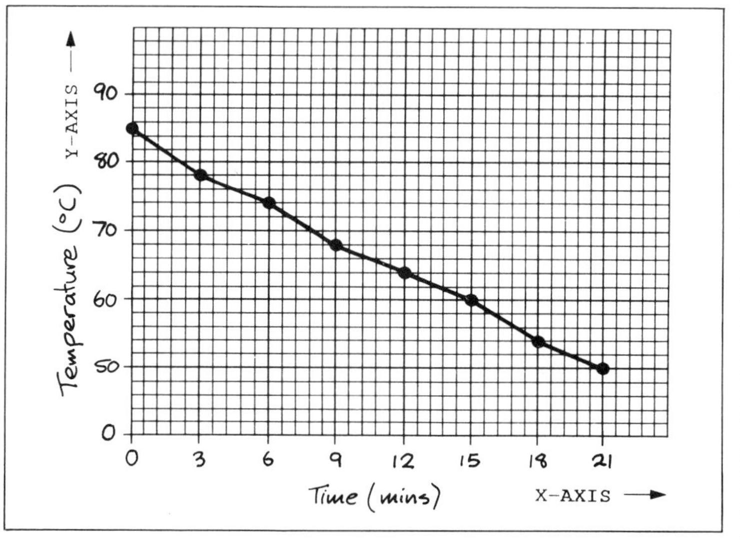

TIME DOWN TO 50 DEGREES 21 mins

Fig 3.4
Cooling tea

independent variable and the changing **temperature** of the tea is the **dependent variable.** In plotting graphs, you must remember that the horizontal, or X, axis is always reserved for the independent variable (in this case, time); and the vertical, or Y, is reserved for the dependent variable (in this case, temperature).

Many students often choose the wrong axes when constructing graphs, although John got it right this time. Even more of them express the opinion that the choice of axes is arrived at purely by guesswork, change or even intuition! If there are two axes, they are commonly known as the horizontal and vertical axes. Since the so-called 'vertical' axis doesn't rise vertically out of the paper, it is better (and more mathematical) to call them the X and Y axes respectively. To remember which is which, just think to yourself – 'X is a-cross and so the Y must go up the page'. One further tip worth remembering is that **time** is **traditionally** plotted on the X axis, whatever kind of variable it is!

As you have seen, it is fine for the experimental variables to change during the experiment. But there are other variables that **must not change.** These other variables are termed **fixed variables** and should be kept as constant as possible. Here are some of the fixed variables for the tea cooling experiment detailed previously:

- The amount of tea in the cup (it is not safe to drink in the lab!).
- The same thermometer should be used for each temperature reading.
- The temperature of the lab should be kept constant (don't open all the windows and doors half-way through the experiment).

You can probably think of a few more and will have realised by now that *all* of them could affect the outcome of the experiment to a greater or lesser extent. In planning and carrying out our experiments we have to be realistic; it can be very difficult to keep *all* the fixed variables constant throughout the experiment. In our example, the cooling rate of the tea could be affected by 'atmospheric pressure', but we would not easily be able to control that variable! In biological experiments or investigations that are carried out in the field, it is even more difficult to ensure that the fixed variables remain stable. Such 'controls' are best achieved in a laboratory.

4.2 Controls

Ideally all the experiments that you carry out should be **controlled experiments** in which you, as the scientist, try to alter only *one* variable at a time. Often a **control experiment** is set up to check this. In simple terms, a control experiment is a second experiment, identical to the first one except for the one variable being investigated. In a properly controlled experiment, you should be able to show that the variable under investigation is responsible for the results you get.

An example should make clear what is meant by controls. This experiment concerns the effect of surface area on the rate of a chemical reaction. In a chemical reaction one of the reactants will often be a solid and the other a liquid. This is the case in the standard reaction to make carbon dioxide gas, which is produced when hydrochloric acid reacts with calcium carbonate (marble chips):

$$CaCO_3(s) + 2HCl\,(aq) \rightarrow CaCl_2(aq) + H_2O(l) + CO_2(g)$$

The **question** to be answered is: Does the surface area of marble chips affect the rate of this reaction?
The student's **hypothesis** might be: The size of the marble chips has no effect on the rate of the chemical reaction.
The **apparatus** used to measure the rate of the reaction is shown in Fig 3.5.

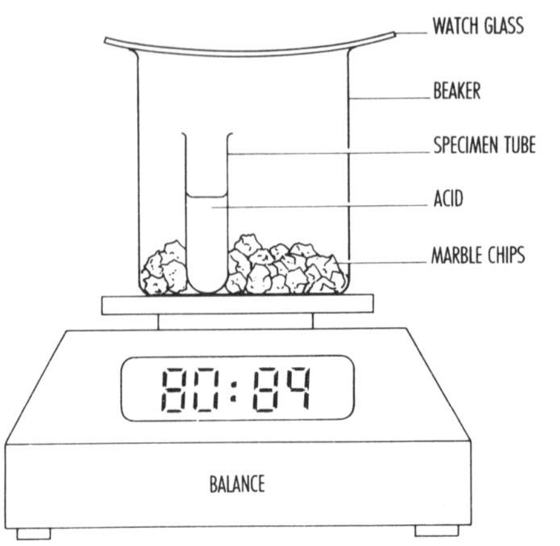

Fig 3.5
Marble chip apparatus

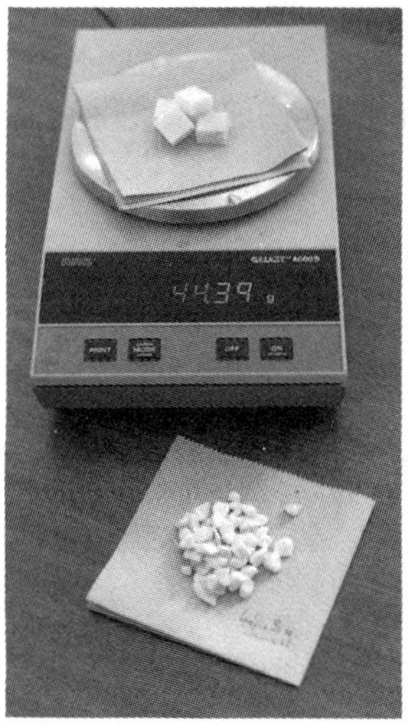

Marble chips and lumps

The **method** followed could be written after rough planning and should be similar to this:

A known mass of normal large marble chips and a small specimen tube containing a known volume of acid are placed in the beaker. A watch glass is placed on top of the beaker to prevent the escape of any liquid during the reaction. Next, the beaker and its contents are weighed. The specimen tube is then tipped over to let the reactants mix. The stop watch is started at the same time and the mass of the whole apparatus is noted at every minute until there is no further loss in mass.
(Note: The carbon dioxide can escape between the watch glass and the beaker lip and so the beaker gets lighter as long as the reaction continues, so by weighing the beaker the rate of the reaction can be followed.)

The experiment is repeated twice and everything is kept **exactly the same** each time **except** the **surface area** of the marble chips:

A For the control experiment the 'normal' large chips are used. The surface area is the total area of all the chips;
B For the experiment the **same mass** of marble chips is used, but they are very much smaller ones and so have a much greater surface area.

The **results** must be recorded in a table like the one below:

Time mins	Mass of A in g	Loss in g of A	Mass of B in g	Loss in g of B
0	20.0	0	20.0	0
1	19.5	0.5	19.0	1.0
2	19.0	1.0	18.4	1.6
3	18.6	1.4	18.1	1.9
4	18.3	1.7	18.0	2.0
5	18.2	1.8	18.0	2.0
6	18.1	1.9	18.0	2.0
7	18.0	2.0	18.0	2.0

To build the table you will need to find the loss in mass at different times. If you are fortunate, your electronic balance will let you zero it with the empty beaker, watch glass and specimen tube on, so that the only mass you read is that of the acid and the marble chips as above. If it does not, simply record the total mass of the apparatus and chemicals; the mass of the apparatus will not change so you need not worry about it! The loss in mass at any time will equal the starting mass *minus* the mass at that time. All you do then is plot the loss in mass for the experiment and the control against time.

The graph should look something like the one in Fig 3.6.

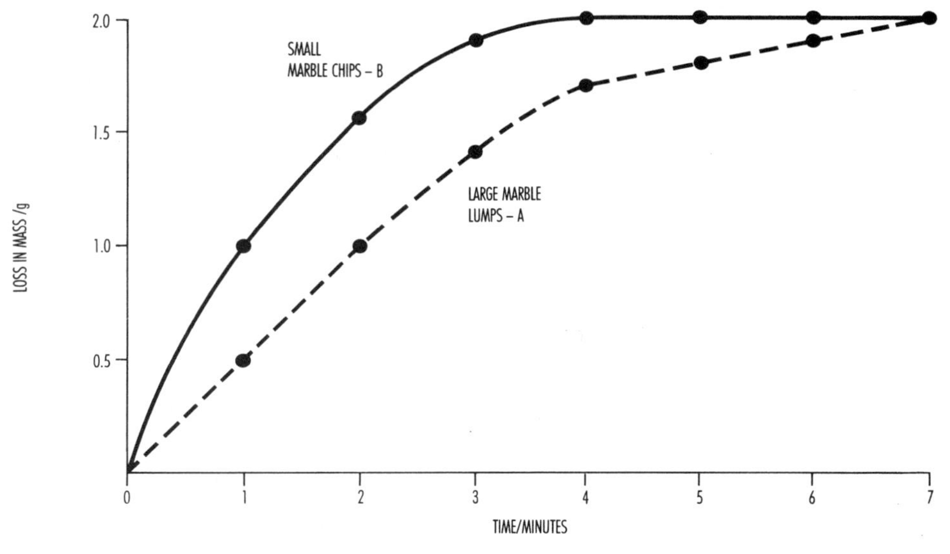

Fig 3.6
Marble chip reaction rate graph

In **discussing** or **concluding**, you should review the results table and graph, and then make important observations, such as:

- The reaction in experiment B is much faster than in the control experiment A; the steepest curve shows the fastest reaction.
- For the large marble chips the reaction lasted 7 minutes, whereas when small marble chips were used the reaction was complete in 4 minutes.
- The final loss in mass was the same for both A and B, which indicates that the reaction was the same in each case, producing 2.0 grams of carbon dioxide gas.

Finally, you need to return to your **hypothesis**. In this instance the investigation shows that when you changed *only* the surface area of the chips, the reaction was speeded up. So now you must *reject* your hypothesis because it does not fit your observations. This is not a failure, it is a success! It needs re-writing to fit your findings:

New hypothesis: the size of marble chips does affect the rate of the chemical reaction with the rate increasing as the size decreases.

Now let us review our variables:

- The *independent variable* was the variable the experimenter changed – the size of the marble chips.
- The *dependent variable* was the variable changed by the experiment – the rate of the reaction (measured as loss in mass!).
- All the *other variables* must be *controlled* by the experimenter – they must not change!

Here are some of the variables that must remain *fixed* if the test we have devised for this hypothesis is to be a fair one:

“Some examples of fixed variables.”

a) Same beaker, specimen tube and watch glass.
b) Clean, dry and empty to start.
c) No change in room temperature.
d) Same quality (purity) of marble chips in A and B.
e) Same strength of acid in A and B.
f) Same standard of measurement in A and B.
g) Accurate time measurements in A and B.
h) Same electronic balance in A and B.

There may be more variables to control – can you think of any? Do you know why all the ones listed are on the list?

DO I HAVE TO INCLUDE A CONTROL?

Controls are not always needed, as in experiments that are *comparisons* between different situations involving the independent variable. Here, each situation acts as a control for the other, or others. If we chose to do an experiment like the one above, but were investigating the effect of temperature on the rate of the reaction, we would only need to carry out the experiment at *two* temperatures. Any *difference* would be due to temperature, because we would have fixed all the other variables.

DO I UNDERSTAND CONTROLS?

Controls are strange things, but when you grasp the idea, all will become crystal clear! If you still find the idea confusing, text books can be a great help. But your teacher or lecturer is your best resource! If you need help with the design of an experiment you are doing, discuss it with your teacher and sort out what kind of control is needed. You will certainly get help if you ask, because teachers are well aware that students generally find the concept of controls mysterious. But they know that when the ‘penny-drops’, problems soon disappear!

SUMMARY

There are some excellent tips about designing and planning in the suggestions below. The sound advice they give is basically intended to prevent students ‘rushing in’ before they have stopped and thought about the problems they have to solve. They list the things **all** planners are *expected* to do, all **good** planners *should* do, and finally all **really good** planners *will* do. You will find the similar checklist that follows useful as a means of measuring your standard of experimental design:

- All students should:
  a) list the things that have to be done;
  b) have a general idea about how the problem will be solved;
  c) ensure that their plan is a safe one;
  d) be sure that the tests they make are *fair tests*.
- All **good** students will:
  a) be able to think of several ways to solve a problem;
  b) be so well organised that their clear, written plans could easily be followed by others;
  c) draw up tables for results or list any measurements that must be made;
  d) be flexible enough to know that their plan may not be perfect first time.

▶ All **really good** students will:
a) be ready with alternative plans in case a first plan fails;
b) be able to produce plans to solve very complex problems;
c) make sure their results are reliable by taking repeated readings or measurements;
d) build control experiments into their investigations whenever they are necessary.

UNIT 5 EVALUATING EXPERIMENTS: SUGGESTING IMPROVEMENTS

The evaluation of an experiment or investigation is often a new starting point in scientific research (see the 'Scientific Problem Solving Cycle' on page 50). Practical sessions that have been organised for you will often provide new questions for you to solve for yourself. Many of the examples of coursework in Chapter 4 start as 'teacher-organised' and lead into 'student-organised activity', e.g. Units 8, 9, 10 and 11.

Evaluation is an integral part of the process of science. It involves reviewing your original hypothesis in the light of the new evidence acquired (see also Unit 3 of this Chapter). You must then consider whether to accept or reject your original hypothesis. A new or modified hypothesis might be the result of your evaluation.

One college re-organised a GCSE Science topic to allow for a much more ***pupil-centred*** approach. One part of the module involved the class in organising their own 'learning expedition' to a Zoo or Wild Life Park. They chose a nearby Wild Life Park.

The class had to co-operate to organise the whole visit, including transport, insurance, finances, what was laid on for them, times to interview staff, booking cameras (still and video) tape recorders, etc. They did have guidelines, but the task of learning about the 'Variety of Life', 'Characteristics of Living Things' and the 'Essential Requirements for Life' was down to them! The class was told to co-ordinate their research and to stage an exhibition so that all the findings could be shared. This was a new way of working for some, and valuable coursework for many.

Fig 3.7
Wildlife park research

Students and keeper at the wildlife park

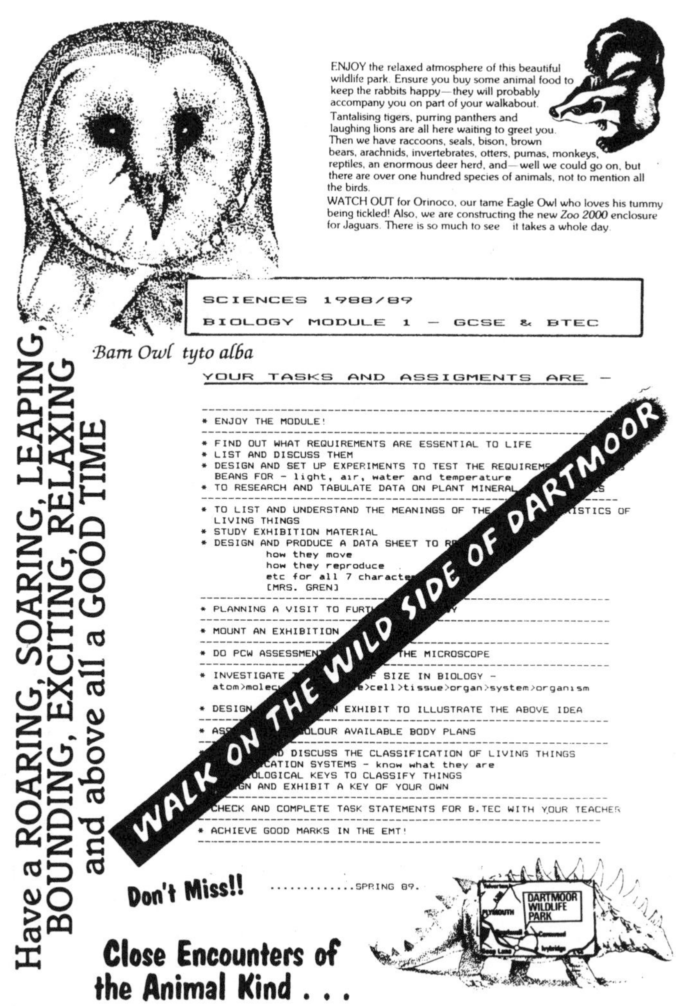

“Planning is a vital ingredient.”

They found the staff very co-operative and were invited to consider long-term scientific investigations at the Park. Most students had planned carefully and were able to complete their intended investigations during the day; but those who had not got clear objectives suffered ‘stimulation overload’ and achieved little on the day. The secret of successful practical science is not to short cut the planning stage! If you do, there will be very little to evaluate.

“Once you have the results, evaluate them and your procedures carefully.”

All aspects of an investigation should receive consideration when you evaluate it; your experimental design, your apparatus, the observations, the recorded data, etc. Often, students discover that the original hypothesis was not as sensible as it seemed, or that the techniques, apparatus and materials chosen were inadequate. Sometimes, the results defy any simple analysis and are too complicated, or too numerous to make sense of. All these difficulties indicate problems with the experimental design process, or that the results do not fit well with the original hypothesis. *Evaluation* means admitting fault, but not failure! You will gain marks for good evaluation. You can suggest improvements, and even re-think the design and/or hypothesis if necessary. You could go on to suggest what you think should be done as follow up.

5.1 How marks are awarded

We will stick to our 6 mark notional maximum again in this section:

- 2 marks – student suggests and uses simple experimental strategy to investigate a given practical problem. Attempts ‘trial-and-error’ modifications in response to the experimental work being done.
- 4 marks – details and carries out a sequence of activities to investigate a given problem. In a situation where there are two variables, recognises the need to keep one constant while the other is being changed.
  Comments critically on the original plan, and makes appropriate changes in response to the experimental work being done.
- 6 marks – analyses practical problems systematically, produces a logical plan and carries out the investigation.
  In a given situation, recognises that there are several variables and attempts to control them.
  Evaluates chosen procedures, suggests and carries out modifications where appropriate and shows a systematic approach in dealing with unexpected results.

5.2 Coursework requiring these skills

Most of the examples in Chapter 4 lend themselves to the assessment of *evaluation*; Unit 11 has an interesting ‘criticism’ section by the student. The trouble with evaluation is that if you are a keen scientist, it is all too easy to get trapped into the ‘scientific problem-solving cycle’. Be sure you are at a convenient point to stop whenever the time runs out!

UNIT 6 ASSIGNMENTS

What are *assignments*? Are they projects? Are they topics? There remains much confusion about this issue. Your teachers will argue that a student-centred approach (giving you responsibility for your learning!) is nothing new. However, what we are *not* talking about is ‘doing projects’ by copying sections out of encyclopaedias, or ‘doing assignments’ by following step-by-step printed instructions.

Have a look at Fig 3.8, which is an assignment ‘recipe’ written by a teacher, giving the students responsibility for the topic ‘Food and Digestion’ within the module ‘HUMANS’. Once this assignment has begun, with a common introduction and experiences, the students have freedom to work within the availability of resources to complete the tasks set.

In this sort of learning situation your teacher will take on more of a ‘tutorial’ role, dealing with students as individuals or in small groups. Because of the initial stimulus sessions led by your teacher you should be able to make an informed choice as to the direction of your research and potential areas of study. The example on 'Food and Digestion' (Fig 3.8) is highly structured, which may help students unfamiliar with the organisational responsibility necessary to be successful in this approach to learning.

SCIENCE STUDY UNIT (MODULE HUMANS)

Topic FOOD AND DIGESTION

1. What do you need food for?
   Task: Complete the questionaire sheet on 'DIGESTION'
2. What is a balanced diet?
   Task: Compare the amount of energy, and nutrients, needed by people of different ages. Refer to table 3 on page 106 'IS'. Also answer questions 1-4 on page 107 referring to table 5.
3. How much energy do you need?
   Task: work through questions 1-4 on page 104.
   Homework: Analyse your own weekly diet to find out how much energy you take in each week.
4. Analysis of food
   Practical investigation: Plan and carry out an experimental analysis of the three food samples to find out if they contain sugar, starch or protein. See sheet titled 'Food Test'.
5. How does food get to where it is needed?
   Practical investigation: Plan and carry out an investigation to show that sugar, but not starch, is absorbed through the gut into the intestine. You will need to refer to Integrated Science book for details. Present a full account of your investigation.
6. How is food digested by enzymes?
   Practical investigation: Plan and carry out an investigation to study how saliva acts on starch, use page 110 IS for guidance. You will need to present a full account of your investigation. If time permits, attempt one of the further experiments suggested.
7. Where does the food go?
   Research: find and draw a large labelled diagram of the gut. Mark on the diagram (i) where pepsin is secreted, (ii) where soluble food is absorbed, (iii) where the pH is acidic, (iv) where faeces are stored.
8. How do enzymes work?
   Research and make brief notes to describe and explain how enzymes help to digest food.
   Draw diagrams to show large molecules of starch being changed to small molecules of glucose.
9. How does food get to the muscles?
   Research and then draw a flow chart to show how soluble food molecules get from the gut to your muscles. Which organ receives all the food from the gut?
10. Energy from food
    Practical assignment: Plan and carry out an investigation to compare the amount of energy released when a peanut burns, to that released when bread or biscuit burn.
    How will you make a fair test to compare the energy released?
    Present a full report of your investigation. Page 112 IS may help.
11. How much energy do you need?
    During the last two weeks you have been monitoring your weight as an indication of how much food you have eaten and not used as energy.
    List 5 things which will affect how much energy you need.
    Explain to someone who has put on weight why they have got heavier.
    Why does an elderly person need to take extra care with their diet?
    Find out what is meant by the term 'hypothermia' and how it can be prevented. (ref: elderly people, mountaineers, swimmers).
12. Food additives
    Using the food labels you have collected, work through the unit on Food Additives in the SATIS folder.
13. Band aid/Sport aid/etc etc.
    Discuss the main issues involved in supplying food to people who are starving. Present a short essay summarising the main arguments for and against the idea of sending food from countries which have a surplus.

Fig 3.8
Assignment: food and digestion

Assignment-based learning can take place outside the laboratory. You will therefore have an opportunity to link with the 'outside world', the whole school, home, industry, commerce and your community. In this realistic learning situation, a whole variety of skills can be acquired or improved. Your social skills and personal confidence are sure to receive a boost. One aspect that you might find exciting is the opportunity to negotiate with your teacher how you should go about the study within the broad framework of the assignment.

You, with your teacher, might be attempting to assess or profile how your learning and skills are developing. Such information might form part of your whole school profile or Record of Achievement (if your school or college already runs such a scheme). Through such means your personal tutor and parents might share your progress in science. The following are just a few of the wide-ranging skills that might be enhanced during assignment-based work, and which might form part of your 'achievement' when you leave secondary education. Your ability to:

"Skills involved in assignment-based work."

- Tackle an appropriate problem
- Analyse the nature of a problem
- Identify, consult and use appropriate reference sources
- Initiate, develop and then communicate ideas and proposals as an individual or part of a group
- Apply any relevant knowledge
- Decide upon an appropriate solution
- Plan/organise the resources you need
- Organise a program of study to meet a deadline
- Monitor your own progress and share your view with your teacher
- Evaluate the quality and efficiency of your learning
- Focus your learning, discriminating between the relevant and the irrelevant
- Reading skills
- Writing skills
- Talking and listening skills
- Research skills
- Picture skills

In assignment based work your teacher will often encourage you to involve other subject areas in your science. Departments such as Home Economics, CDT, Technology, Geography, Mathematics and others may already be involved in so called 'cross-curricular' work because this is part of your school or college policy. This will certainly be so if TVEI (Technological Vocational Education Initiative) funding has reached your area, as it will all areas in the next few years. It may also bring 'joint accreditation', where some of your GCSE Science coursework might automatically count towards a BTEC or similar qualification.

In establishing guidelines for assignments, specific *objectives* will have been identified for you. These are 'stepping stones' by which you may progress towards achieving long term *aims* – and ultimately your GCSE. Objectives ar supposed to be short term and realistic. The guidelines for the 'FOOD and DIGESTION' example include many of these. That sheet was designed to help students plan their work and to appreciate the sum of their achievements. You will probably enjoy this style of learning which is likely to become increasingly important over the next few years.

CHAPTER 4

EXAMPLES OF STUDENT COURSEWORK

UNIT 1 INTRODUCTION

This chapter contains typical examples of coursework produced by students studying for double and single GCSE Science awards. The examples have been chosen to provide a comprehensive coverage in terms of both *content* and *skills*.

The examples that follow each make up one Unit of this chapter and have a common format. Each is divided into sub-sections, as shown below.

- **Syllabus link**
  This explains the context of the coursework example within a Science course, in terms of both *theory* and *practical* applications.
- **Cross-references**
  The coursework samples are arranged in units which correspond with the chapters of the Longman 'Revise Guide: GCSE Science'. If you do have access to that book, these *cross-references* (X-ref) will help to reinforce your learning and understanding with more detail.
- **Coursework task**
  This is a brief outline of how instructions were given to the student and the form that the practical session took.
- **Possible skills assessed in coursework**
  Each piece of coursework will involve a very wide range of practical skills. However, in setting up the coursework task, the teacher or lecturer will have focused on one or two of the most appropriately assessed skills. The particular skills assessed will depend on a variety of factors; the task itself, the Examining Group whose syllabus is being followed, and the student's practical ability. Some of these skills cannot be 'seen' in written accounts, but would be observed and recorded at the time.
- **Typical student's coursework**
  The samples of coursework that follow are based on work produced by real students as they studied for the GCSE Science. Any changes that have been made are only intended to maintain the anonymity of the original writers and to make their work a little clearer to you, the reader.
- **Examiner comments**
  These comments from the teacher/examiner are intended to highlight good work, or to point out features which might be improved upon. It is not common practice for teachers, examiners or moderators to write such comments on the coursework which you produce.
- **Examiner assessment**
  There are no actual marks given in this section because the schemes used by different Examining Groups vary considerably. Also, the original assessments may have included skills which were observed *during* the practical session, rather than on the final written account handed in by the student. Only *general comments* are made, though there is a broad indication of the standard achieved.
- **Further suggestions**
  The suggestions made include ideas for the further development of the particular coursework assignment, together with other related practical activities that might be linked in some way. Each of the suggestions might well involve additional practical or presentational skills that might be assessed. It is important that you appreciate that a very broad range of *teacher-organised* practicals are possible within each area of a Science course. This section might also provide support for you in *student-organised* practical assignments.

UNIT 2

GETTING STARTED

2.1 Weather maps

This is the first coursework example and has been selected because it is relatively simple. It is designed to test whether the student can **interpret information**. It also shows that it is possible for some assessments to take place *outside* a laboratory if one is not available. Alternatively, if a Satellite Weather Station has been established in the school or college, the weather information used can be obtained first hand by the student.

Satellite weather map

- **Syllabus link**
  Understanding the relevance of science to everyday life is a feature of the GCSE courses, so the scientific interpretation of weather maps is included in many science schemes.
- **Cross-references**
  Revise Guide; GCSE Science pp. 141-5.
- **Coursework task**
  In the weather map illustrated in Fig 4.1, the low pressure shown 200 miles to the west of Devon and Cornwall is expected to pass over these counties within the next 24 hours. What detailed weather forecast would you broadcast on Radio Devon?
- **Possible skills assessed in this coursework**
  Extracting data (Chapter 2, Unit 6.1); Recognising patterns (Chapter 2, Unit 6.3); Drawing Conclusions (Chapter 2, Unit 6.4).
  In this simple example symbols are used rather than numeric data, such as temperatures, pressures and wind speeds.
- **Typical student's coursework**

“The interpretation of the isobar and wind direction is correct.”

“The consequence of wind speed related to isobar spacing is also shown.”

```
The forecast is:
The winds will be from the west. They
will go faster from the south west. It
will get much warmer.
```

“There is some misinterpretation assuming the exact correlation of wind direction and isobars.”

Fig 4.1
Weather map

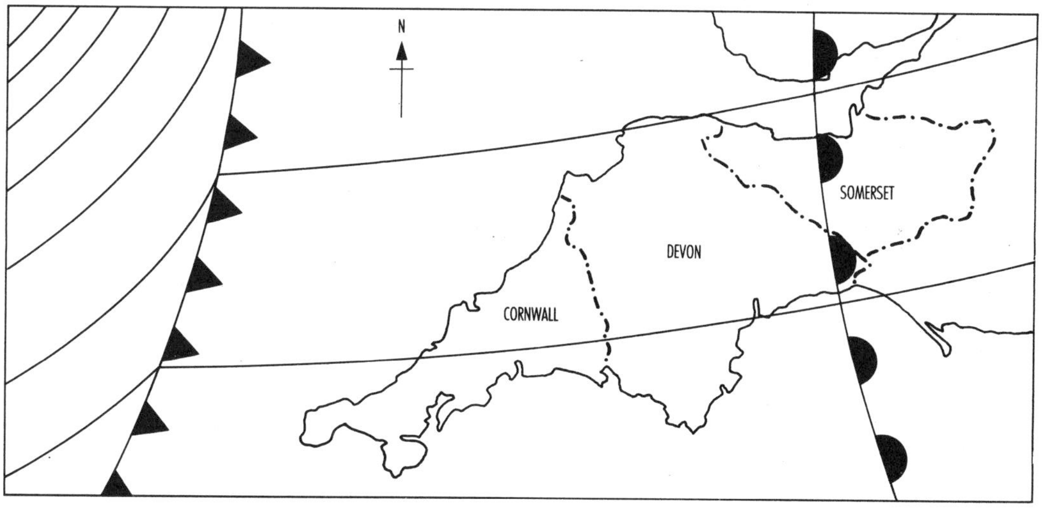

Examiner comments
Poor piece of work. The student's account is too brief and good observations are not developed. The interpretation as a weather forecast could have been more thoughtfully organised, with the audience and radio transmission in mind.
Clearly the front has little meaning to the student. Even if interpreted correctly as a *cold* front, there is no evidence of development of the interaction between cold and warm air masses and precipitation. The warm front has almost passed over Devon and the weather pattern will have been one of increasing wind and cloud cover, light rain or drizzle and a fall in pressure. As the cold front passes, the rain will become much heavier, the wind will become very strong and the temperature will fall. Finally, the pressure will rise and as the rain ceases the sky will clear.

Further suggestions
This coursework task: something more like a weather forecast could be written; the student's work in the example lacks both detail and awareness of the audience.
Related work: some further work using newspaper and T.V. forecasts would increase the student's ability to interpret and draw conclusions from a weather map or a synoptic chart. The potential for student-organised research would be great if students had access to satellite weather maps 'downloaded' through a school computer system, and could operate the system themselves.

UNIT 3 ENERGY AND FUELS

3.1 Measuring food energy

Syllabus link
One of the most important topics in the study of GCSE Science is the study of energy and fuels. Fuels are full of energy and it is energy that can make things happen. Before your science lessons you should make sure that you have some food – brains need energy to do work!

Energy crops up throughout science in several different disguises. These are called the forms of energy and they fall into two major groups:

i) *Potential energy*, such as mechanical, chemical, gravitational, magnetic, nuclear and heat.
ii) *Kinetic energy*, such as that in moving objects, waves, electricity and heat energy (which you will notice appears in both groups).

Whatever form of energy you are considering it will be measured in joules (J). Energy is often changed from one form to another by an 'energy transducer'. These include such things as the retina of the eye, which changes light energy (electromagnetic waves) into electrical energy (nerve impulses), and an electric light bulb, which does the opposite by changing electricity into light (and some heat!).
Fuels hold great interest for us as we rely upon them for both our quality of life and very survival. Because our fuel supplies are finite (they will eventually run out) scientists and technologists are actively investigating 'alternative energy' sources such as solar energy, water and wind power. Such investigations can form the basis of interesting student-organised practical work. The practical exercise shown in this coursework occurs very

commonly and so is dealt with in some detail. It concerns the 'release of energy' from foods, which in living things is achieved through the process of respiration. Outside the bodies of living things we talk of burning, combustion and oxidation.

Cross references

Revise Guide; GCSE Science pp. 11–25, pp. 91-2.

Coursework Task

This coursework task involves burning a known mass of food and using the heat energy released to increase the temperature of a known mass of water. From the data obtained, it is possible to calculate the energy content of the food in joules per gram.

Two examples of this task are given; each was presented differently by teachers in different schools.

Task given in school A

The students were given access to a selection of laboratory apparatus which included all the basics, plus anything they could negotiate the use of with the teacher. Selection of equipment was an important part of the teacher's plan for assessment. Students were then asked to measure the heat energy released on burning peanuts and calculate the potential energy per gram, at the same time recording carefully what they had done. Previous lessons had already covered the necessary practical and theoretical background. Finally, they were required to re-design their apparatus, explaining how they would further reduce errors in their results.

Task given in school B

The students were given a *worksheet* (see below), which structured the exercise very clearly, but still offered the opportunity to consider the design of apparatus.

The written evidence of both versions can be seen in the 'Typical student's work' section below.

WORKSHEET — GCSE SCIENCE PRACTICAL

POTENTIAL ENERGY — FOOD

AIM To find out how much chemical energy is stored in 1g of peanut.

METHOD

By burning the peanut you can release its chemical energy store as heat and light. If you use this energy to heat up some water and see how much hotter the water gets you can find out how much energy is stored in the peanut. You must design the experiment, but you will need the following –

a) a peanut mounted on a needle
b) a measuring cylinder (10cm^3)
c) a boiling tube and holder
d) a thermometer
e) access to an electronic balance

QUESTIONS/TASKS

1 Draw the apparatus to show how you have used each piece (5 marks).
2 Record your results as indicated:
Mass of peanut =
Mass of water =
Starting temperature of water =
Final temperature of water =
Temperature change of water =
(15 marks)
3 Using the formula you have been given, work out the energy value of your peanut per gram (3 marks).
4 There are many reasons why this investigation is not very accurate. List as many as possible (3 marks).
5 If you could use any apparatus you like, design an improved experiment to compare the food values of several different nuts (4 marks).

Possible skills assessed in this coursework

Following instructions – written or spoken (Chapter 2, Unit 2.1 or Unit 2.2); Selection and handling of apparatus and materials (Chapter 2, Unit 3); Quantitative observations (Chapter 2, Unit 4.2); Measurement (Chapter 2, Unit 4.3); Recording and communication

(Chapter 2, Unit 5); Processing data (Chapter 2, Unit 6.2); Following safe working procedures (Chapter 2, Unit 7); Designing an experiment (Chapter 3, Unit 4) and Evaluating an experiment (Chapter 3, Unit 5).

Burning a peanut

▶ Typical student's Coursework

“Clearly the pupil has not drawn the apparatus he used. Diagram is poor and badly labelled.”

“Most students used the recommended $10cm^3$ of water; with a large peanut this small amount would have boiled, resulting in dramatic heat loss.”

“The calculations are correct, but not shown and again no units.”

“No consideration of the mass of the peanut and so does not really complete the task set.”

“No idea of measurement checks, more samples, taking averages, elimination of heat losses etc.”

Student in school A

1 RESULTS

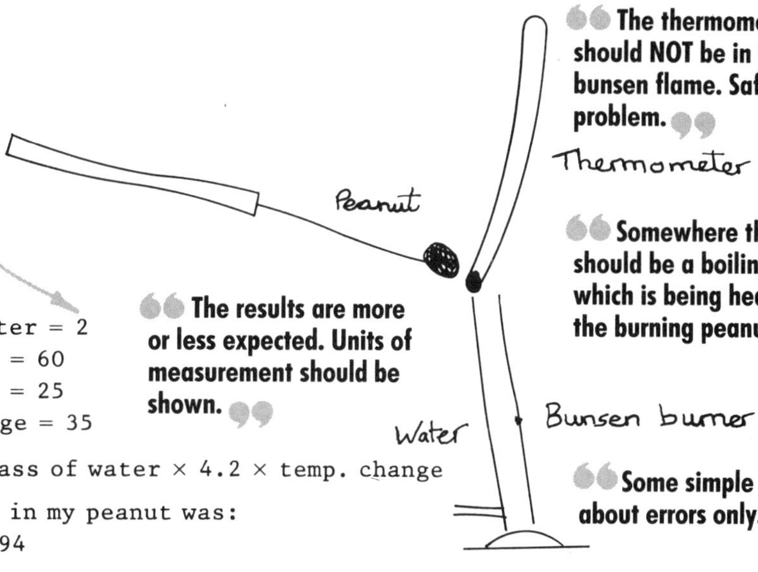

“The thermometer should NOT be in the bunsen flame. Safety problem.”

“Somewhere there should be a boiling tube which is being heated by the burning peanut.”

Mass of water = 2
Final temp = 60
First temp = 25
Temp. change = 35

“The results are more or less expected. Units of measurement should be shown.”

Energy = Mass of water × 4.2 × temp. change

The energy in my peanut was:
Energy = 294

“Some simple ideas about errors only.”

My experiment could be inaccurate because incorrect measuring or thermometer might be wrong.

To get it more accurate I would get a better thermometer.

Student in school B

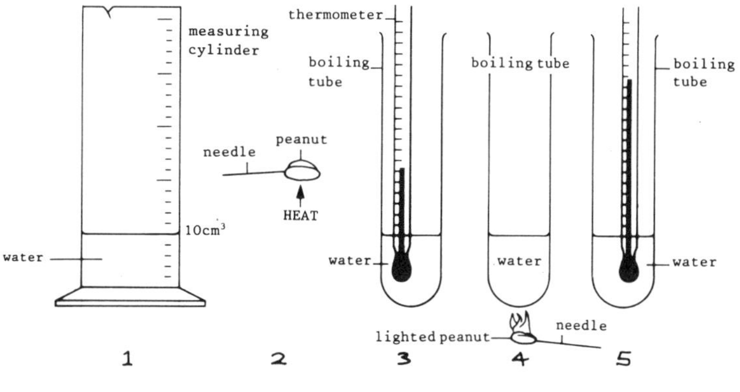

“The drawings could have been larger and might have illustrated the method more clearly. They do, however, show how each piece of apparatus has been used.”

2 RESULTS

Mass of peanut	0.45g
Mass of water	10g
Final temp. of water	58°C
Starting temp. of water	21°C
Temp. change of water	37K

Excellent. Neat, clear results table. Clever use of Kelvin units for temperature difference – correct, but not expected. All units shown. Starting temperature for tap water seems rather high, this could be an error.

Good. The formula is stated correctly as is required and the transfer of the data is shown clearly. The calculation is correct and energy units are included.

3 ENERGY VALUE

Using the formula given – $\frac{\Delta t \times s \times mw}{mf}$ = ENERGY VALUE (J)

Where Δt = Temp. change (K = degrees Kelvin)
s = Specific heat capacity of water = 4.2 J/g
mw = Mass of water (g)
mf = Mass of food (g)

Substituting the data collected $\frac{37 \times 4.2 \times 10}{0.45}$ = 3453.3 J/g

The energy value of the peanut tested was 3453.3 J/g or 3.45 KJ/g.

The concluding line is a sensible addition, particularly as the units are changed to make the result more manageable and perhaps more meaningful.

4 REASONS why this experiment is not accurate:

Energy can escape while lighting the peanut.
Energy can escape while heating the water.
Some energy has to heat up the glass boiling tube.
Putting in a thermometer could lower the temperature.
Light energy is not measure.
There is some sound energy, but it is very little.

The reasons given are all appropriate. The fourth shows realization that all parts of the apparatus take up heat and should be included in the calculation. The sixth point provides evidence of very careful observation – this student is using all her senses.

An intention to use several nut samples of each type is very sound practical science.

5 Improved experiment:

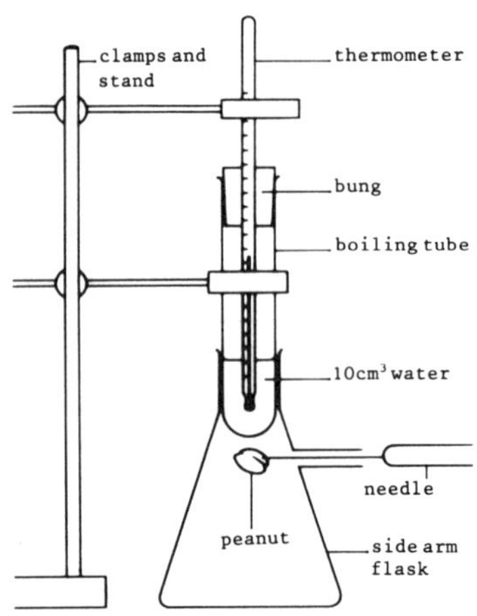

APPARATUS. My re-designed apparatus is shown in the diagram.

METHOD. The method would stay the same, but each different nut type should be tested more than once and an average for each obtained. Nuts of the same type look and taste differently so they may also vary in energy content.

The improved experiment shows an understanding of the new task, but a lack of design skill. The list she made above should have provided help, but the need for oxygen and the difficulty of lighting the nut seem to have been overlooked.

More detail of the new method would have been useful.

EXAMINER COMMENTS

Student A's work is **poor**. Many important and desirable features of experimental work are absent, such as correct representation of equipment used, units of measurement, clearer idea of sources of error and some real 'thinking' behind the design. Did this student really know what was going on? Was this the student who did nothing in his group and so had no understanding of what was being done, or why?

Student B's work is of a **moderate** to **good** standard. Different parts of the exercise have been carried out at different levels of performance. Drawing of diagrams and design skills certainly still need some attention. There were also some opportunities that she missed such as:

a) There was soot deposited on the tube.
b) Food samples did not burn completely.
c) Could any of the measurements have been inaccurate?
d) Why did she not repeat the test on the peanut in the first experiment?

FURTHER SUGGESTIONS

This coursework task: comparisons of the amounts of energy released on the combustion of both fuels and other foods could be investigated. Any food or fuel that will burn might be used. Comparisons of the same foods treated in different ways, such as fresh, roasted, and honey-roasted peanuts would produce interesting information. The effect of wick length on a candle heat energy output would also provide an interesting investigation, particularly if measurements of light energy output were also made.

Related work: other forms of food testing would be useful and could easily include tests for starch, reducing and non-reducing sugars, proteins, fats and oils etc.

UNIT 4

CURRENT ELECTRICITY

4.1 Electrical Power

- **Syllabus link**

An electric current is a flow of charged particles through conductors around a circuit. In fact it is the flow of negatively-charged electrons from negative to positive in the circuit. Strangely though, convention encourages us to think that the flow is from positive to negative.

You must make yourself familiar with basics such as series circuits, parallel circuits and the symbols used in circuit diagrams (Chapter 2, Unit 2.3). In order to make a success of practicals you must master at least the use of the electrical meters which are used to measure volts (potential difference) and amps (current).

The practical exercise dealt with in this Unit relies on the student's understanding of the previous lessons that have dealt with electrical 'power' which is measured in watts (W). A watt is one joule of energy per second, the rate at which energy is used. One watt of electrical power is a very small quantity, so one thousand watts, or 1kW, is a much more convenient amount to consider. The electrical appliances in your home will have power ratings clearly marked on them. A 60-watt light bulb uses 60 joules of energy per second, or more correctly changes it into different forms! The practical exercise in this Unit allows the student to investigate the relatonship between the current flowing through a heater and its power output.

- **Cross references**

Revise Guide; GCSE Science pp. 26–41.

- **Coursework task**

The task was presented by the teacher as an introduction to dealing with electrical power (watts) and does not rely upon the student knowing about the relationship between current (I), voltage (V) and power (W). The particular skill that was being assessed was that of 'experimental design and execution', though many other skills could have been assessed using this exercise.

The task was presented in the form of a worksheet:

WORKSHEET GCSE SCIENCE PRACTICAL

CURRENT ELECTRICITY — POWER

PROBLEM

If the current flowing through an electrical heater is doubled, is the power (i.e. heat output per second) doubled also?

APPARATUS etc.

Power supply	Thermometer
Heating element	Beaker
Ammeter 0-5A	Water
Variable resistor	Stopclock
Leads	

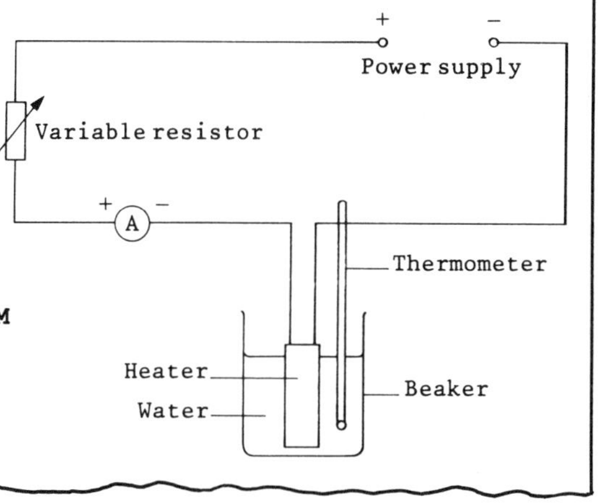

CIRCUIT DIAGRAM

INSTRUCTIONS

Decide how you will use the apparatus provided to solve the problem and answer the question stated above, then carry out the experiment. There is no penalty (this time!) for incorrect wiring of the circuit, so if you are at all in doubt ASK YOUR TEACHER TO CHECK IT.

On the A4 paper provided, put your own name and your teacher's name. Write a description of the method you have used, record all your results and show how you have used them to reach your conclusion (answer to the question). Mention also any problems you encountered (and how you overcame them) and any sources of error which may have affected the reliability of your experiment.

Possible skills assessed in this coursework

Following instructions – Written (Chapter 2, Unit 2.2); Diagrams (Chapter 2, Unit 2.3); Selection and handling of apparatus (Chapter 2, Unit 3); Observing and measuring (Chapter 2, Unit 4); Recording and communication (Chapter 2, Unit 5);
Interpreting information – Recognising patterns (Chapter 2, Unit 6.3); Drawing conclusions (Chapter 2, Unit 6.4); Identifying the problem and planning the investigation (Chapter 3, Unit 2); Designing an experiment and an appropriate control (Chapter 3, Unit 4); Evaluating the experiment and suggesting improvements (Chapter 3, Unit 5).

Testing an electrical heater

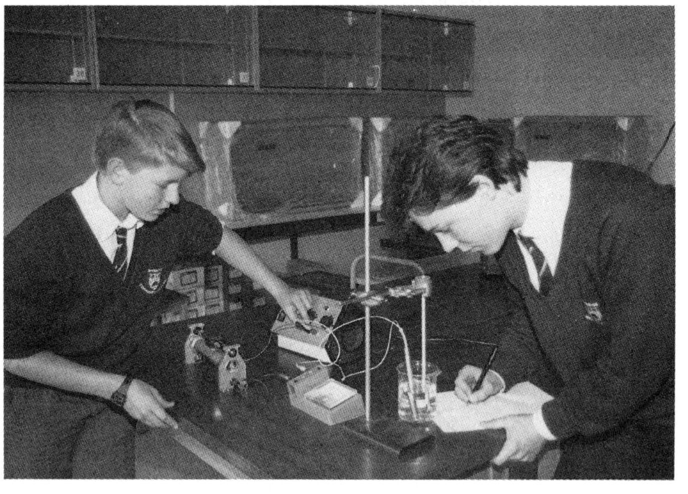

Typical student's coursework

Name – Wayne Teacher – Mrs Dalglish
Problem: If the current flowing through the heater is doubled, is the power doubled?
Method: Set up the apparatus as shown in the diagram on the worksheet.
Get teacher to check the apparatus for wiring errors.
OK ✓
Put the thermometer into the water and time how long it takes the water to heat up through ten degrees celcius.
First of all use the current as 2.5A and time how long it takes to heat the water, then repeat the experiment exactly with the current reduced by half to 1.25A.

Results

Temp. of water at start (°C)	Current (A)	Time taken through 10°C
15°C	2.5A	6 mins. 47 secs.
25°C	1.25A	11 mins. 57 secs.

Conclusions The answer to the questions is probably yes.
When the power is doubled so is the current (approximately).
If the current is reduced so is the power.

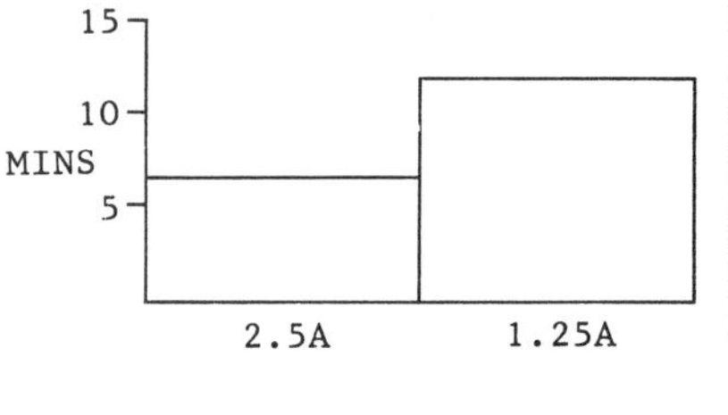

Method is basic and lacks essential detail – a good method should provide all the information needed for some-one else to repeat the experiment.

Good. Getting teacher to tick a box confirming circuit is correct.

Results clear and well presented, but much data is missing.

Units don't need repeating in columns, time would have been more meaningful, and scientific, in seconds.

Bar chart a good idea, but conclusion soon becomes confused. The student doubled the current and measured time for a fixed temperature rise. Here it is suggested that the power was doubled by the student.

Idea is sound and should produce reasonable results.

Good. Plan to exactly repeat the experiment with half the current.

Sadly, results show the starting temperature of the water was different in the second experimental run. Rate of heat loss is proportional to the temperature difference between a hot body and its surroundings. So more heat loss errors on higher temperature run.

No problems? If there are marks for identifying them, admit to some however small they were!

Not many particular errors identified, but shows fundamental understanding of the idea of controlling variables.

```
Bar chart of power
* I decided to heat the water the 5°C instead of 10°C to save time.
Discussion
I had no problems. Errors could creep in if measurements are hurried or
badly read from the clock and ammeter. Both experiments must be exactly
the same except for the current flowing, any difference would be an
error.
```

EXAMINER COMMENTS

Moderate standard of work. The student conducted the experiment fairly well, but could have improved the records and the reliability of the results obtained. What has been produced is quite well presented. It is unfortunate that the conclusion is confused, it illustrates the need to read through what you write to ensure that what you say makes sense in relation to **your own** results.

In this particular experiment the teacher was using a check list to make the assessment fair. In this student's case it would have to be adapted, as the method chosen was not the one expected. Twenty marks were available and were awarded as follows:

Method

First run	*Second run*
initial temp. noted 1	initial temp. noted 1
current noted 1	2 x current noted 2
mass/vol. noted 1	same mass/vol. 1
final temp. noted 1	final temp. noted 1
heating time noted 1	same heating time 1
temp. rise 1	temp. rise 1
mention of stirring 1	

States that heat produced is proportional to temperature rise 2.

Conclusion and Discussion

States **valid** answer/conclusion to question from actual results 2.
Sensible comments on problems/errors one mark each (max 2) 2.
Total out of 20 marks. Can be scaled for the Exam Groups mark requirement for this skill.

FURTHER SUGGESTIONS

This experiment: vary the starting temperature to see if it affects the result at the same current. This will establish whether this variable affected the results the student obtained in the experiment detailed above. Other variables could be controlled also, heat loss by insulating the beaker for instance.

Care: when working with water and electricity! **Safety** must be considered at every stage.

Related experiments: similar experiments may be carried out with a lamp in a simple circuit; by using a voltmeter and an ammeter, the power output of the lamp can be calculated. This alternative technique using the Power = Current × voltage formula is another way to answer the question about the relationship between current and power. It would give some interesting results.

Linked work: the use of correct fuses in electrical appliances and the buying of electricity all involve power calculations.

UNIT 5 ELECTROMAGNETISM

5.1 Electromagnets and transformers

▶ **Syllabus link**

When an electric current passes along a wire it creates a *magnetic field.* If two magnetic fields interact, then movement takes place. This is how movement is created in an electric **motor**, which combines the effects of both electricity and magnetism.

Even more simply, an electric current flowing through a coil of wire has the effect of making the coil act as a *magnet*, but when a soft iron core is added an **electromagnet** has been made. These are used in all sorts of machines, from scrap-metal moving cranes to telephones.

Transformers incorporate an interesting reversal of the opening sentence. If electricity produces magnetism, is the reverse also true? Can magnetism be transformed into electricity?

A transformer is a simple device that does both these things. One side of the transformer, the *primary coil*, changes electric current into magnetism. Inside the coil is a soft iron core which acts as a guide for the magnetism, carrying it to the *secondary coil*. As the magnetism flows past this coil it is changed back into electricity.

Transformers only function when magnetic fields keep changing, and will only work with an alternating current. By altering the number of turns on the two coils, transformers can be made to increase (step-up) or decrease (step-down) voltage and current values.

Electromagnetism is one aspect of science that has many applications in everyday life. The practical exercise in this Unit is intended to increase the student's understanding of electromagnets and transformers, as well as provide opportunity for the assessment of two skill areas. Firstly, 'measurement and observation', and secondly, 'the use and organisation of equipment'.

- **Cross reference**
  Revise Guide; GCSE Science, pp. 42-52.
- **Coursework task**
  Involves the making of electromagnets and transformers, and is fully explained in the worksheet (below) provided by the teacher:

WORKSHEET GCSE SCIENCE PRACTICAL

ELECTRICITY — ELECTROMAGNETS & TRANSFORMERS

INTRODUCTION

In this exercise you will be asked to investigate the performance of an electromagnet and to construct a transformer.

APPARATUS etc.

Westminster power supply	1 lamp (6V, 0.3A)
2 C-cores	4 leads
2 lengths of wire (2m and 4m)	Sheets of card, iron and aluminium

Answer sheet on which to record what you **observe** and **measure**.

METHOD

1 With the 2m wire doubled back on itself wind 10 DOUBLE TURNS onto one C-core. Connect the ends of the wire to a source of DC (probably red and black terminals). Show the apparatus to your teacher **before** you switch on. Bring up the second C-core and investigate the force required to separate the cores (see diagram A).

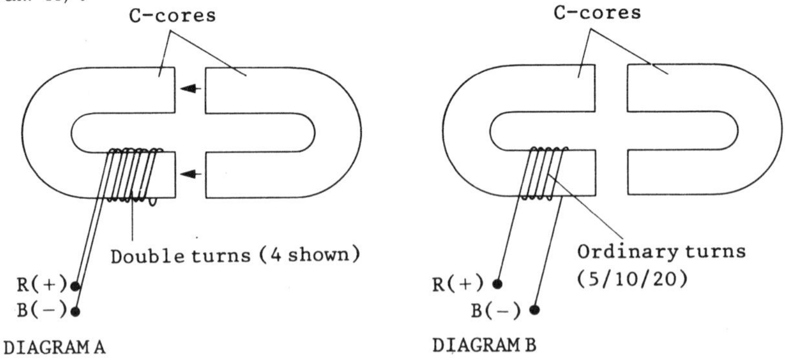

2 Remove the DOUBLE TURNS and wind onto one core:
a) 5 ORDINARY TURNS
b) 10 ORDINARY TURNS
c) 20 ORDINARY TURNS

In each case bring up the second core and investigate the force required to separate the cores (see diagram B).
Explain any difference between the effects seen in 2(b) and 1.

3 Using the 20 turn coil and a source of DC, investigate the effect of inserting sheets of card, aluminium and iron between the cores (see diagram C).

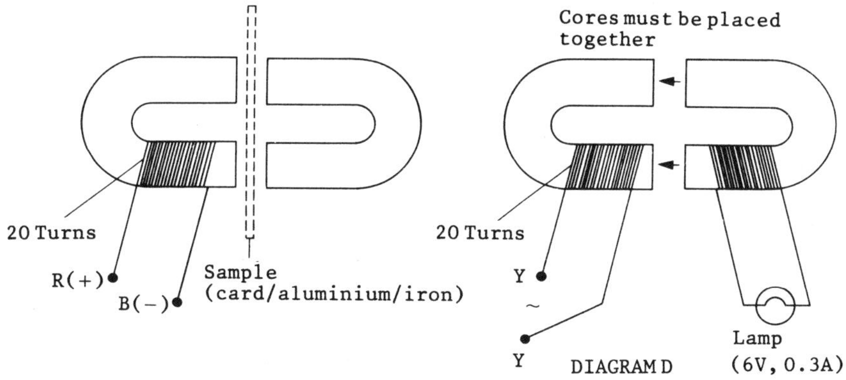

4 Connect the 20 turn coil to the AC terminals (probably yellow). Describe and explain what happens when the cores are placed together.
5 Now connect the lamp to the AC supply. Does the lamp light? Do you think that there is any current flowing through the filament of the lamp?
6 Connect the 20 turn coil to the AC terminals and wind sufficient turns of the 4m length of wire onto the second core to **just** light the lamp. Record this number of turns (see diagram D).
7 What is the effect of winding more turns on the second core (try three or four times as many as you used in 6)?
8 Rewind the coil as in stage 6 and connect it to the AC terminals on the power supply and the 20 turn coil to the lamp. Does the lamp light? Explain what is happening.

▶ **Possible skills assessed in this coursework**
Following instructions – Written (Chapter 2, Unit 2.2); Diagrams (Chapter 2, Unit 2.3); Selection and handling of apparatus (Chapter 2, Unit 3); Observing and measuring (Chapter 2, Unit 4); Recording and communication (Chapter 2, Unit 5).
Interpreting information – Recognising patterns (Chapter 2, Unit 6.3); Drawing conclusions (Chapter 2, Unit 6.4).

ANSWER SHEET SCIENCE GCSE

ELECTROMAGNETS AND TRANSFORMERS

ANSWERS TO QUESTIONS

1 Effect of 10 "double turns" on core

It doesn't work at all.

“ Better to have said something about the force such as – no significant force needed to separate cores. ”

2 Effect of "ordinary turns" on core

a) 5 turns when power is switched on, the force is quite strong to pull away the magnets. The magnet vibrates.

“ Small force required. ”

b) 10 turns with 10 turns, it is impossible to pull the magnets apart.

“ Larger force required. ”

c) 20 turns with 20 turns, it is again impossible to pull the magnets apart.

“ Very large force required. ”

Difference between 1 and 2b) with 10 double turns the magnets did not go together, but in 2b. The magnets were impossible to get apart.

“ Good. Difference clearly indicated. ”

3 Effect of sheet between cores

Card There is some magnetism, but you can pull the two magnets apart quite easily.

“ Card – Two points really should have been noted, the card was not attracted and force was weaker than in 2c. ”

Aluminium – Again two points, the aluminium was not attracted and the force was much weaker.

Iron – The iron was attracted and the force was very weak, almost negligible.

Good – all points noted!

Good, though 'dim' rather than 'dull' was the word to use. Explanation sufficient, though not clearly stated.

Good. For a maximum score 7, 8 or 9 turns must be recorded.

Excellent.

Well explained, though a mention of 'step-up' transformer would have improved it.

Aluminium The magnets do not attract each other because of the aluminium.

Iron The magnets attract, and so does the iron. The force is exactly the same as without the iron.

4 Effect when 20 turn coil connected to AC

The magnet vibrates alot, and the magnets attract strongly, but it is not very easy to pull them apart.

5 Lamp connected to source of AC

Brightness of lamp
Current flowing: YES/~~NO~~
Explanation

The lamp is quite dull, because the current wasn't flowing through the bulb it wouldn't light.

6 Minimum number of turns = 7 turns.

7 Effect of increasing number of turns (in 6)

The lamp glows brighter with more turns as more current is there.

8 Effect of connecting "new coil" to source of AC

Brightness of lamp Quite bright. Brighter than before.
Explanation This is because the more turns on the magnet, the stronger the current going through the lamp.

EXAMINER COMMENTS

As far as 'observation and measurement' skill is concerned the student's written record was **good**. A little more careful thought before writing might well have improved the way the answers read. It is important to remember that others might not understand what you mean. Be brief, be clear and stick to the point.

The 'use and organisation of equipment' skill was assessed by the teacher using a checksheet with each one of the following checks being worth 1 mark for the student:

a) Winds non-inductive turns
b) Energises the coil
c) Constructs e/mags. with 5/10/20 coils
d) Investigates effect of card, Al and Fe separators
e) Investigates effect of AC
f) Connects lamp to AC
g) Connects 20 turn coil to AC
h) Increases turns in small steps
i) Shields lamp to check for min. emission of light

This student did actually score 9 out of the 10 possible marks and so **very good** describes her performance in this skill area. Such a score could easily be scaled to fit any Exam Group assessment scheme.

FURTHER SUGGESTIONS

This investigation is comprehensive and provides good background to an understanding of electromagnetism and transformers. The use of laminated (many thin sheets of iron) and non-laminated (solid iron) C-cores could be investigated if they were available. Laminations are said to increase the efficiency of the transformer. Some interesting investigations into voltage could be done by adding a CRO to the equipment list.

Related experiments: it is quite simple to build electric motors either from a kit, or 'odds and ends'. They can be used to investigate the effects of various changes on the speed of the motor, such as the strength of the magnetic field, the level of current and the number of coils on the core. These would all provide interesting information.

There are some fascinating applications of *moving magnets*. The magnetic strips on the back of credit cards and British Telecom Phonecards create minute electric currents when moved past a sensitive 'read-head'. The electrical signal is then converted into a number code. Surely, here is an opportunity for some student-organised investigation into 'plastic-money'.

UNIT 6

WAVES

6.1 Reflection – ripple tank

Syllabus link

You will probably remember a number of different sorts of wave, including sound, water, radio and X-rays. Although there are two main types of wave, longitudinal and transverse, all waves share the ability to **transfer energy from one place to another**. All waves have other measurable characteristics: speed, frequency and wavelength are three key ones. The relationship between these is given by the 'wave equation/formula':

Speed = Frequency × Wavelength
(units m/s) (units Hz) (units m)

If you know any two, the third can be calculated using the equation.

One other word is often used to describe a wave, and that is **amplitude**. In a water wave the amplitude would describe how much the wave rises and falls. In a sound wave with a large amplitude more energy will be carried, and it will be louder than a sound wave with a small amplitude. Amplitude describes how much **energy** is carried by a wave. There are whole branches of science devoted to particular kinds of wave, and the range of possible practical work is enormous.

In the school or college laboratory **ripple-tanks** are often used to investigate the behaviour of water waves, which illustrate principles that apply broadly to all forms of wave.

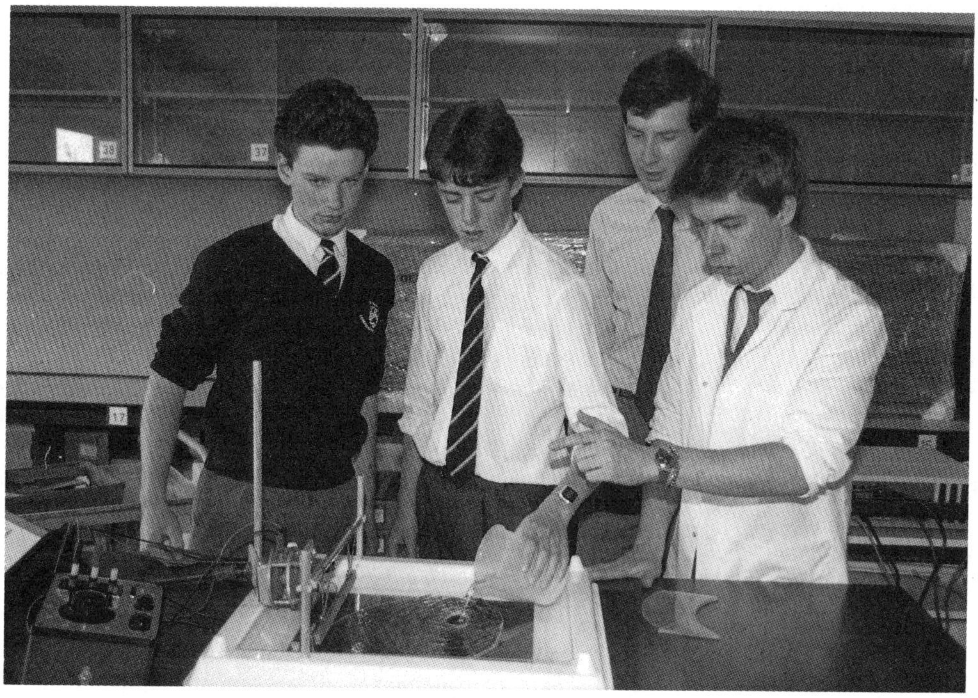

Ripple tank in use

The ripple-tank provides a convenient model with which to investigate **reflection** and **refraction**. These effects can easily be seen in shadow patterns under the ripple-tank. A third effect, **diffraction**, can also easily be demonstrated using the ripple-tank. In the piece of coursework shown, students were asked to work in small groups. They had already had some practical experience of waves using a 'slinky spring', lengths of rubber tubing, a model wave machine and a laser. The ripple tank exercise formed an introduction to the 'laws of reflections'.

Cross-references

Revise Guide; GCSE Science, pp. 53–63.

Coursework task

The teacher explained the functioning of the ripple-tank and demonstrated its use to the class. It was stated that this simple apparatus allows us to study waves that we can see. Because, although we can see light and hear sound, we cannot make out individual waves. Water ripples are easy to see, their behaviour can be observed and measurements can be made.

This pre-written transparency was then placed on the overhead projector (OHP):

WORKSHEET GCSE SCIENCE PRACTICAL

WAVES — REFLECTION

WHAT TO DO

1 Using a ripple-tank and working in groups, set up a vibrating beam to produce straight waves.
Once you have a steady supply of such waves, place a straight metal barrier at an angle (as illustrated) to the movement of the waves.

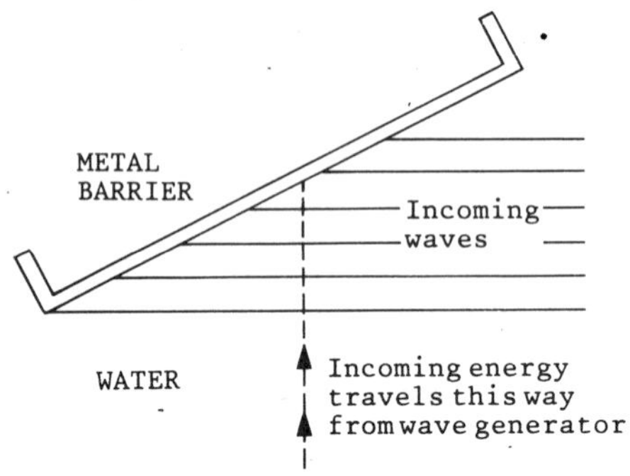

Watch what happens – record your observations carefully.

2 Devise and carry out an experiment to find out if there is any pattern in the way the waves behave after striking a straight obstacle at different angles.

Write up your experiments individually and hand them in at the end of the lesson.

The class then dispersed into working groups of three for the practical session.

Possible skills assessed in this coursework

Following instructions – Written (Chapter 2, Unit 2.2); Diagrams (Chapter 2, Unit 2.3); Selection and handling of apparatus (Chapter 2, Unit 3); Observing and measuring (Chapter 2, Unit 4); Recording and communication (Chapter 2, Unit 5).
Interpreting information – Recognising patterns (Chapter 2, Unit 6.3); Drawing conclusions (Chapter 2, Unit 6.4); Working with others (Chapter 2, Unit 7); Identifying the problem and planning the investigation (Chapter 3, Unit 2); Designing an experiment and an appropriate control (Chapter 3, Unit 4); Evaluating the experiment and suggesting improvements (Chapter 3, Unit 5).

Typical student's coursework

WAVES - reflection

INTRODUCTION

This is a practical using a ripple tank in the dark. The water waves in it act like lenses which focus a pattern of light on the floor. The pattern is the same as the waves in the tank.

1. We set up the ripple tank and after a while got some steady straight waves. When we put a straight metal barrier in the way the waves hit the barrier and bounced back. There were waves all over the place bouncing off the sides and mixing together.

2. AIM
To find out if there is a pattern to the way waves behave after striking a straight obstacle at different angles.
APPARATUS
The ripple tank, two metre rulers and a protractor.
METHOD
We did the same as in the first part but we measured the angle between the line the waves were moving along and the barrier before and after they bounced off. To do this accurately we put pieces of paper on the floor for each angle and put the rulers in line with the way the waves moved or bounced. After doing five angles we stopped and transferred our results to a table. We made pencil marks where the rulers and barrier had been put each time. I measured the angles and wrote them down.

“Good start, the student is well organised and explains what the patterns on the floor are.”

“Simple observation only, how did the waves bounce back? Angle? Size? Still a straight line? Other reflections from the sides interesting, but a nuisance?”

“An error not to have added a simple drawing as on the OHP, but with reflected waves added.”

“Clear and well structured experiment, aim taken from task given and re-stated. Good.”

“Apparatus brief, again unsupported by a diagram which would have improved communication. No mention of the necessary power supply.”

“Method is good, but not sequential. A re-write in some 'order of doing' would make it easier to repeat.”

“Some very good ideas within the group. The paper sheets and the rules for instance.”

Sadly it is not clear what angles were measured, neither one of the group's five sheets nor a diagram was included in the write up. This will become important later as the meaning of 'angle of incidence' and 'angle of reflection' are used in a theoretical context.

RESULTS

Angle of Wave	Angle of Bounce	Difference
45°	46°	1°
30°	28	2°
20°	20°	0
10°	11°	1°
60°	60°	0

CONCLUSION

I think that the pattern is if the waves hit the obstacle at any angle they bounce off at the same angle. It was difficult to measure the angles of the waves accurately so the results could be one or two degrees out easily.

Pattern identified and margin of error allowed for – good.

Results clear, could be improved by putting units at top of column not on each entry, except where it got forgotten. Difference column was a bright idea.

EXAMINER COMMENTS

This is a **good** piece of work spoilt by a lack of drawings or diagrams to support and extend the text. With such additions it would have been very much better. There was an interesting change from 'we' to 'I' during the write up, which may indicate a leading role for this student within the group of three. The group did not use the hand stroboscope that was available to them. It may have helped solve the problem of identifying the exact angles in which the waves moved. No mention was made of the very confusing results generated as the different waves in the tank overlap each other.

FURTHER SUGGESTIONS

This experiment: this was a very basic experiment concerning the 'laws of reflection', but only dealt with reflections at straight surfaces. Reflection at concave and convex surfaces could be investigated in a similar way. At a concave surface the incident straight wave, which is rather like a parallel beam of light, is converged to a focus as a circular wave. Water waves behave the same way as other waves in this respect. In a solar cooker the sun's heat is brought to this focus at the 'cooking point', where the food must be placed. At a convex surface the reflected wave spreads out, or diverges.

Related experiments: would include the use of the same apparatus to investigate **refraction**, **diffraction** and **interference**.

UNIT 7

FORCE AND MOTION

7.1 Measuring 'g'/Hooke's Law

- **Syllabus link**

Whenever you see something moving, a **force** (pull, push or turn) will be responsible. It takes time when things move from place to place and some journeys take longer than others. How long a journey takes depends on how quickly the distance is covered. We use the terms **speed** and **velocity** to describe this. They are very similar, but velocity must always show in what direction travel is taking place. They have the same units, that include miles per hour (m.p.h.) and kilometres per hour (km/h) which are used in our every day lives, and the laboratory units of metres per second (m/s) and centimetres per second (cm/s).

As well as the idea of an **average speed** (or velocity) that stays constant for the whole journey, we have the possibility of **acceleration** (speeding up) and **deceleration** (slowing down). Such changes in speed are measured over a set time period and the most common unit used for this change is m/s^2 (m/s per second).

The force of **gravity** is one of the first forces that we explore as babies, when we drop food from our high-chairs or toys from our prams. When we release an object on Earth it begins to accelerate downwards.

One of the two pieces of coursework here shows how a pendulum can be used to measure the acceleration due to gravity (approx $10m/s^2$). The other piece of coursework illustrated is unusual in style, but is one of the commonest practical exercises in this area of science. It concerns forces in **balance**. When two or more forces are balanced, nothing moves. The 'spring balance' or 'newton meter', that you might often use in a laboratory, works in this way. The extension (stretch) of the spring inside it gives an idea of how heavy an object might be. You may be familiar with **Hooke's Law** which explains this behaviour of a spring or elastic band.

- **Cross-references**

Revise guide; GCSE Science, pp. 64–75.

- **Coursework task**

Task A

This takes the form of a highly-structured exercise which was intended to allow the assessment of two skill areas, 'Following instructions' and 'Drawing conclusions from experimental observation and data'. This method of finding the acceleration due to gravity is the least 'high-tech' one available, but can be very accurate. The worksheet based practical session (see Fig 4.2) was intended to support the theory work being done at the time.

WORKSHEET GCSE SCIENCE PRACTICAL

FORCE AND MOTION – gravity

Measuring 'g' using a pendulum

SKILL [i] 1 2 3 4 MARKS NAME __________
SKILL [v] 1 2 3 4 MARKS

INTRODUCTION
The study of the pendulum was originally made by GALILEO who had noticed the swinging of a lantern suspended from a roof. By using the beats of his pulse, Galileo discovered that the time for a complete swing was always the same. He was probably the first person to consider their use in accurate clocks.

The period (T) is the time taken to make a complete swing (to and fro). The period of the swing, T, depends in general on the length, L, of the pendulum. It can be shown that -

$$T - 2\pi\sqrt{\frac{L}{g}}$$

where g is the acceleration due to gravity at the place where the pendulum is used. This formula for T is true only if the pendulum swings to and fro through a VERY SMALL ANGLE.

T is in seconds, L is in m and g in m/sec^2

The formula can be re-arranged so that g is the only thing you can't simply measure -

$$g = \frac{4\pi^2 x L}{T^2}$$

So you need to find T and L very accurately, then use a calculator to work out g.

I suggest you measure the pendulum very carefully to the nearest mm and find T by working out the average time for one swing. You can do this by timing 50 swings and dividing your measured time by 50 to get the time for a single swing.

You might try calculating g two or three times for different length pendulums; you could then work out an average value for g which might be quite accurate!

TASK - 2/3 MAX PER GROUP.
Devise a way of measuring 'g' in this lab. Carry out the investigation writing it up fully!

Fig 4.2
Finding 'g' – pendulum method

APPARATUS AVAILABLE CONFIDENTIAL____________

Thread Drawing pin A 'bob' (weight) A stop watch A ruler

Lined paper Stool/chair/table from which to hang pendulum

HINTS L = length of pendulum (m) π = 3.14 T = Time for 1 swing(s).

LENGTH OF PENDULUM [m]	TIME FOR 50 SWINGS [s]	T = TIME FOR ONE SWING = $\frac{S}{50}$	$g = \frac{4\pi^2 x L}{T^2}$ [m/s²]	g m/s²

MY AVERAGE VALUE FOR g IS ________

Task B

This task is unusual as you will see when you first look at it, but is designed quite specifically to show whether a student can 'handle experimental data'. It is also odd in that a laboratory is not needed during the assessment, which makes it very attractive as a 'top-up' type assessment for students who might have been absent. It was presented in the form of the worksheet shown in Fig 4.3.

WORKSHEET GCSE SCIENCE PRACTICAL

FORCE AND MOTION – Hooke's law

A student, who was investigating the stretching of a spring for different loads recorded his results in the table below.

Conkklueshum.

I wus carrfull and did not bosted the Sprin but carnt sea eny patun.

REED	INS
IN	16mm
5.0	3N
2	34.101mm
400g	67mm
0N	0mm.
6Kg	102
700g	119m

Problem (for you!)

Criticise the way in which the student presented his results; re-draw the table so that any pattern could be seen more easily. What was the pattern and how could it be checked?

Fig 4.3
'Reading' – an unusual coursework task

- **Possible skills assessed in this coursework**

  Following instructions – Written (Chapter 2, Unit 2.2); Selection and handling of apparatus (Chapter 2, Unit 3); Observing and measuring (Chapter 2, Unit 4); Recording and communication (Chapter 2, Unit 5).

  Interpreting information – Recognising patterns (Chapter 2, Unit 6.3); Drawing conclusions (Chapter 2, Unit 6.4); Working with others (Chapter 2, Unit 8); Evaluating the experiment and suggesting improvements (Chapter 3, Unit 5).

"Write up neat and quite well laid out."

"Fixing of pendulum to bench in diagram indicates two possible sources of error.
a) String rubbing on bench slowing down the pendulum.
b) Incorrect length measurement of pendulum if diagram is accurate. String from bench bottom to drawing pin not included."

"Sentences long and over complicated, stick to simple clear ones. Better not to mention Karen by name. All in the group should share this work by double checking any complicated calculations."

"Good. Results table copied clearly and own results entered neatly. Substitution of data into equation shown – helps the examiner see where errors occur, helps the student avoid them!"

"Good. Conclusion concise and relates to information given on the worksheet. Excellent attempt at evaluation. Perhaps a new heading 'discussion' would have been more appropriate for these comments."

▶ Typical student's coursework

▶ Task A

MEASURING 'g' USING A PENDULUM

AIM
To measure the acceleration of gravity.

METHOD
We hung our pendulum over the edge of the bench fixing them by a drawing pin on the side so that they could swing free. We measured the time for 50 swings using the stopwatch for 3 pendulums and put the results in the table copied from the worksheet. Karen then got her calculator out and we worked out the time for one swing and then g in m/s^2. Last we worked out the average value of g.

RESULT

LENGTH OF PENDULUM IN [m]	TIME FOR 50 SWINGS [s]	T = TIME FOR ONE SWING = $\frac{s}{50}$	$g = \frac{4\pi^2 \times L}{T^2}$ [m/s^2]	g m/s^2
0.9	96	1.92	$\frac{4\times\pi^2\times 0.9}{3.69}$	9.63
0.6	78	1.56	$\frac{4\times\pi^2\times 0.6}{2.43}$	9.75
0.3	60	1.20	$\frac{4\times\pi^2\times 0.3}{1.44}$	8.22

MY AVERAGE VALUE FOR g IS → $\frac{9.63+9.75+8.22}{3} = 9.20 m/s^2$

APPARATUS

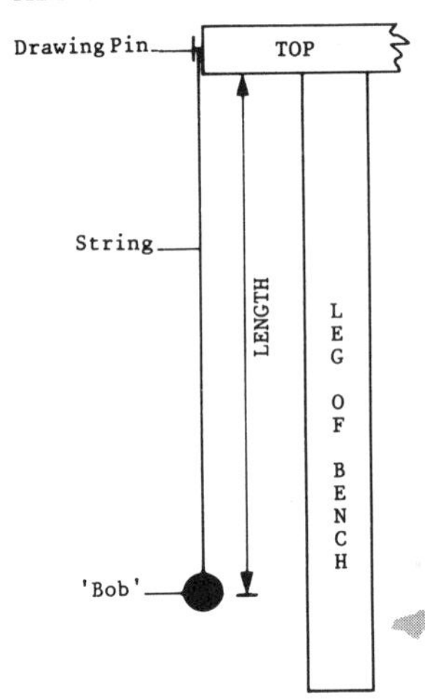

CONCLUSION
The average value for g was 9.2 m/s^2 which was very close to the value given at the top of the worksheet. We think that our times could have been more accurate and that the air might have slowed down the pendulum a bit. It was also easy to miss counting a swing so our result seems quite good considering.

"Diagram fair. Is it accurate? It could have been larger. Was there a floor?"

▶ Task B

Name –

PRACTICAL ASSESSMENT

The student has not used one type of measuring and has used many different types. Also the readings are all over the place, some on one side and some on the other.

This should have been labelled clearly.

"Columns are headed correctly now."

"Correct units have been added, but rather over enthusiastically. If column heading includes units, don't add them to every reading as well!"

"Good. One set of units per quantity now, mixed units have been sorted out by conversion. Excellent. Re-ordering of loads from small to large."

READINGS:

weight used (g)	distance spring moved (mm)
0 gram	0 mm
100 gram	16 mm
200 gram	34.1 mm
300 gram	50 mm
400 gram	67 mm
500 gram	– mm
600 gram	102 mm
700 gram	119 mm

“Pattern is clearly stated, though some more thought might improve the wording!”

“Hooke's Law states that (The extension of a spring is directly proportional to the load force applied as long as the elastic limit is not exceeded.)”

“Good. Graph axes labelled and sensible scales used! Points correctly plotted and best line drawn.”

“Graph not used well, student should have stated how the graph shows the pattern.”

The table should look like this, but different measurements could be used eg:– instead of grams, Newtons could be used and instead of mm, centimetres could be used. I also notice that the student missed out 500 grams which he should have done.

The pattern is that there is a steady increase in the length of the spring and the load put on. This can be seen by looking at the graph I have drawn.

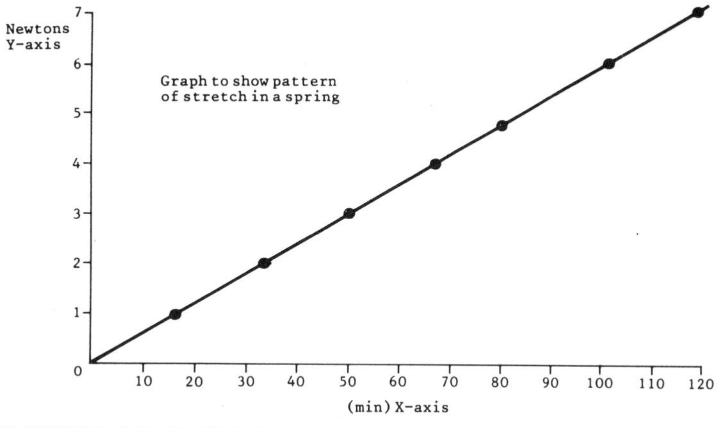

EXAMINER COMMENTS

Task A – **moderate** standard of work. The written sections could be improved with more structured thinking before writing. The method needs more detail if it is to be a repeatable exercise. Listing the things done in order is a good way to start planning a write up of your method. The drawing of the apparatus should be large and accurate, not tucked away in a bit of spare space that needs filling. The group was successful, so there is more to be assessed than a written product. Such things as ‘working with others’ might well be assessed by the teacher during the practical session.

Task B – **moderate/good** piece of coursework, although the student could have commented on the need to use a ruler to draw the chart. The student managed to identify most of the important faults in the ‘specimen results’ provided. Some more thought before writing might have made the criticisms a bit clearer. Although the graph was very well drawn, it was not well used to establish the pattern.

FURTHER SUGGESTIONS

These experiments: Task A – acceleration due to gravity can be investigated in several ways, using ‘multiflash photography’ on a falling object, a ball bearing and electric stop clock device, or a ‘ticker-tape’ timer being just three of them.
Task B – ends itself to practical investigations of springs and elastic bands up to and beyond the ‘elastic limit’. It offers opportunity to compare elastic materials.

Related experiments: such as those into velocity and acceleration using ‘ticker-timers’, trolleys and inclined planes (slopes) provide an opportunity to generate ‘velocity-time’ graphs. The interpretation of these is always easier, once a student has actually produced some practically.

UNIT 8 FEEDBACK AND CONTROL

8.1 Investigating negative feedback

- **Syllabus link**

Biological, physical and chemical systems usually need to be stable and controlled, that is in a state of **homeostasis**. If any of your biological systems become unstable you will be ill, and possibly die unless **control** can be regained. Body temperature and blood sugar level are good examples of factors that need to be controlled if you are to stay fit and well. There are at least three components necessary to control any system:

i) a **receptor** or **sensor** needed to detect any change from the normal or set value;

ii) a **control mechanism** or **comparator** is needed to activate whatever will correct the situation;
iii) an **effector** or **actuator** is needed to do the correcting.

Negative feedback is the means by which control is achieved. All systems that we want to control will consist of **inputs** and **outputs**. In an **iron** for example, the input is the amount of electricity and the output is a constant temperature that will not burn the cloth being ironed. To save us the bother of checking the tempeature and switching on and off, irons are fitted with control devices called **thermostats**. We set these to the desired temperature and leave them to do the adjustment automatically. The thermostat acts as both the sensor and comparator; the actuator is the heating element that can bring the level of output back to the set point. The iron is controlled by negative feedback, the feedback 'messages' being:

i) the iron is too hot, **switch off** the current to the heating elements;
ii) the iron is too cold, **switch on** the current to the heating elements.

If the message had been a **positive** one such as 'The iron is too hot, **switch on** the heating elements ', the shirt would have been scorched and there would be trouble!

The example below is a simple practical exercise that helps introduce the idea of feedback and control. In it the **eye** acts as a **sensor**, the **brain** as the **comparator** and the **muscles** of the arm as the **effectors**. Negative feedback results in the loop of wire being moved away from the stiff wire course being followed whenever it is seen to be getting closer. It does need a steady hand and nerves of steel as well! Although many skills could have been assessed by the teacher, they were restricted to 'Following instructions', and 'Drawing conclusions'. Opportunity was built in for student-organised follow up practical work with the equipment that had been built.

▶ **Cross-reference**
Revise Guide; GCSE Science, pp. 76–88.

▶ **Coursework task**
The task was discussed briefly with the students, but followed on from an introduction to the ideas of feedback and control. A worksheet was provided for guidance and the students did their written work on it (see 'Typical Student's Coursework' section below).

▶ **Possible skills assessed in this coursework**
Following instructions – Written (Chapter 2, Unit 2.2); Diagrams (Chapter 2, Unit 2.3); Selection and handling of apparatus (Chapter 2, Unit 3); Observing and measuring (Chapter 2, Unit 4); Recording and communication (Chapter 2, Unit 5). Interpreting information – Recognising patterns (Chapter 2, Unit 6.3); Drawing conclusions (Chapter 2, Unit 6.4); Identifying the problem and planning the investigation (Chapter 3, Unit 2); Designing an experiment and an appropriate control (Chapter 3, Unit 4); Evaluating the experiment and suggesting improvements (Chapter 3, Unit 5).

▶ **Typical student's coursework**

GCSE SCIENCE — COURSEWORK PRACTICAL

WHICH IS YOUR STEADIEST HAND? COULD YOU BE A PILOT?

BUILD THE SUGGESTED EQUIPMENT TO TEST SCIENTIFICALLY WHICH HAND IS STEADIEST — LEFT OR RIGHT.

EQUIPMENT

What is shown in the diagram + anything in the lab. You need:

DESIGN IDEAS

Coordination tester: The piece of wood can be any scrap thick enough to hammer a nail or screw a screw into at each end. Form the coiled wire path from 16-gauge, bare, copper wire. Attach each end of the coil to a nail or screw. To one of the nails, attach a short wire that leads to one terminal of the bell. Attach the other bell terminal to one terminal of the battery with another length of wire. To the second battery terminal, attach a long piece of bell wire that ends in a bare loop, not quite closed, as shown. With this device, the person being tested acts as a switch. The bell will not ring unless the bare loop connected to the second battery terminal comes in contact with the coiled wire to complete the circuit.

“Tester drawn well considering lack of space.”

“Good. Closed loop and pencil improve design of hand held probe.”

“Tape at start and finish a novel design feature. Well done!”

“Excellent. Washer used with screw made guide wire secure and improved electrical contact.”

“Results clear, calculations shown and correct. Numbers convenient?”

“Tester circuit diagram clever and accurate, though unavoidably rather small.”

“Bar chart is excellent, coloured bars (in original) improving visual impact.”

“A very thoughtful conclusion, good links back to teacher's introduction on feedback and control.”

The idea of the test is to challenge someone to move the loop all the way from one end of the twisted wire to the other end without ever touching it. The more complicated the twists in the wire, and the smaller the loop, the more difficult the test is. Failure is marked by the bell ringing.

DIAGRAM — YOUR TESTER

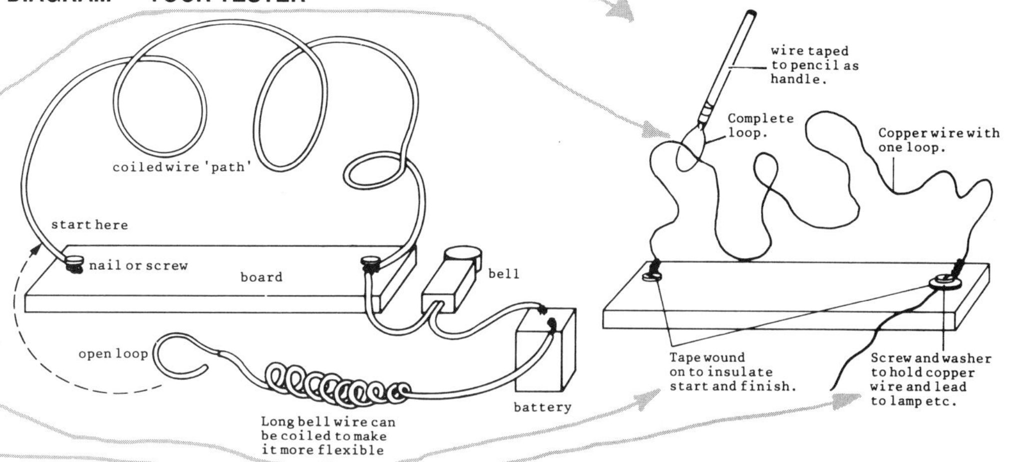

RESULTS TABLE

RIGHT HAND TOUCHES		LEFT HAND TOUCHES	
Test 1 =	3	Test 1 =	7
Test 2 =	5	Test 2 =	9
Test 3 =	4	Test 3 =	11
Average =	$\frac{12}{3} = 4$	Average =	$\frac{27}{3} = 9$

AVERAGE — Add up all three scores and divide by 3.

*TESTER CIRCUIT

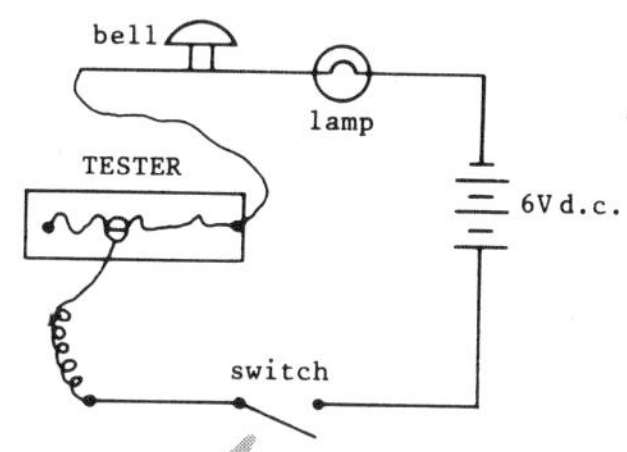

RESULTS BAR CHART

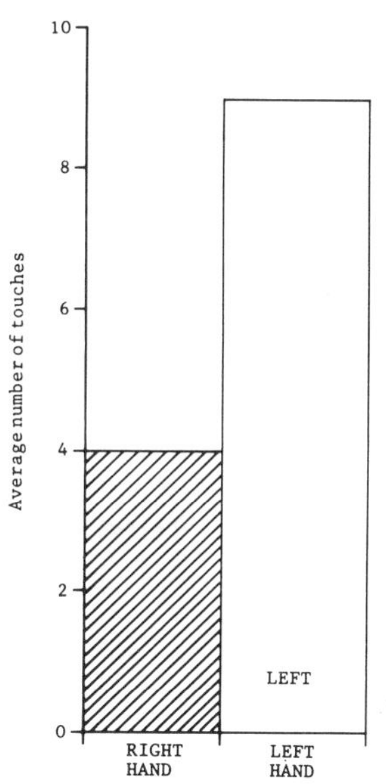

CONCLUSIONS

What did you discover?

The results show that my left hand is much less steady than my right. My right hand is more than twice as good as my left using this tester.

OTHER THINGS TO TEST?

DO OTHER FACTORS AFFECT A STEADY HAND?

AGE
MALE OR FEMALE
EXERCISE
TIME OF DAY

EXAMINER COMMENTS

High standard. This is very clearly a highly structured exercise and one would expect most students to be at least moderately successful. It would be interesting to see the follow-up work using the 'tester' to investigate other factors. Many skills could be assessed when this simple experiment is extended.

FURTHER SUGGESTIONS

This experiment: there are some suggestions on the worksheet for student-organised further study.

Related practical work: electronic and digital control systems such as burglar alarms, smoke alarms, automatic lighting. Biological control systems, blood sugar, temperature and water control (osmoregulation). Mechanical systems such as 'ballcocks', floats in carburettors and bimetallic strip thermostats.

UNIT 9 THE HUMAN BODY

9.1 Food testing

▶ **Syllabus link**

In all science courses there will be aspects of science that apply to you as a human. The food we eat is vitally important for our health. Today it is all too easy to eat the 'wrong' kinds of food. Heart disease and disorders of the digestive system are common in the so-called 'developed countries'.

A healthy and balanced diet can be achieved by eating suitable amounts of the following food types regularly: carbohydrate, fat, protein, fibre, vitamins, minerals and water. In your science course you will learn about these and will investigate foods to find out which contain these essential nutrients.

This practical exercise is about testing for sugars, just one of a range of food tests available in the school or college laboratory.

▶ **Cross-references**

Revise Guide; GCSE Science pp. 89–106.

▶ **Coursework task**

The Benedict's test for reducing sugars was demonstrated by the teacher and discussed by the class. The students were then given a sample of a reducing sugar (glucose) and other 'food samples' labelled A, B, C and D.

▶ **Possible skills assessed in this coursework**

Following instructions – Spoken (Chapter 2, Unit 2.1); Selection and handling of apparatus (Chapter 2, Unit 3); Observing and measuring (Chapter 2, Unit 4); Recording and communication (Chapter 2, Unit 5); Drawing conclusions (Chapter 2, Unit 6.4); Identifying the problem and planning the investigation (Chapter 3, Unit 2); Designing an experiment and an appropriate control (Chapter 3, Unit 4); Following safe working procedures (Chapter 2, Unit 7).

▶ **Typical student's coursework**

FOOD TESTING – Sugars

AIM: To find the reducing sugars.

“Good. Task clearly identified.”

APPARATUS: The apparatus was boiling tubes, bunsen burner, test tube holders, safety spectacles, splints, distilled water, Benedicts solution, some glucose and some unknown foods.

“Probably not necessary to draw diagrams and list apparatus. Waste of time.”

METHOD: We were given some sugar (glucose) with some other unknown foods. We heated the sugar with a few drops of the Benedicts solution until it started to steam, then watched carefully for the result of the test. The result was recorded in the table of results ready to compare with the other foods.

“Good point! Uses test on glucose as a standard.”

With the first result in the rack we tested the other foods in exactly the same way as far as we could and wrote the results into the table.

“Tested each sample in EXACTLY the same way. Excellent scientific method. Only variable is the 'food'.”

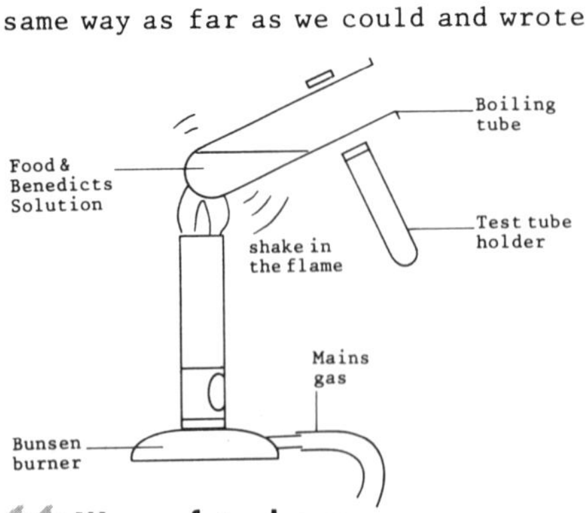

“Diagram showing heating and position of boiling tube in flame and angle gives cause for concern. But student was actually fine when observed in action!”

“Wore safety glasses and pointed tube away from self and others. Tips such as shaking the tube gently in the flame were remembered. Well done, was listening!”

HEATING THE TEST SUBSTANCES

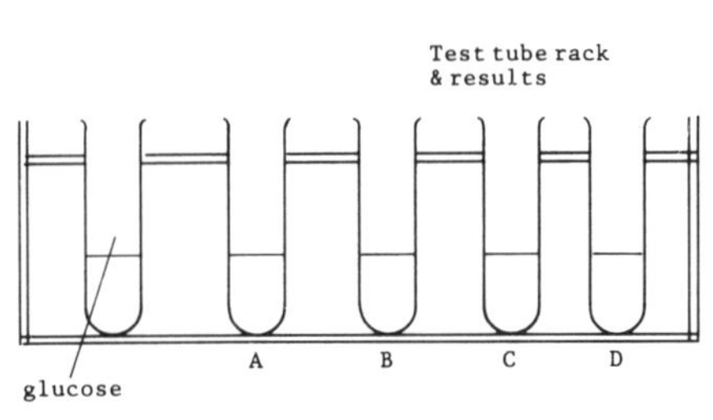

“Tubes with results well organised as shown in the diagram, but could have been stated faster.”

“Results table excellent, perhaps a little more space for observations another time.”

“Use of technical word, precipitate, good.”

“Sugar level key student's own idea. Good thinking!”

“Conclusions match evidence, accurate and clear, but a bit long.”

“Disaster strikes! Private experiments are not allowed! Why were your sandwiches out in the lab.? Danger to others! Good job we are not assessing SAFETY today! Stay and explain after the lesson!”

RESULTS:

Benedicts solution & sample	Observations made on each test	Sugar level xxx or 0
Sugar – glucose	It went pale cloudy green, then bits of orange precipitate sank to the bottom.	xxx
A	It stayed blue.	0
B	It went cloudy, then greenish.	x
C	It went cloudy, then greenish, then orange.	xx
D	It stayed blue.	0

Key to sugar level: xxx – means a lot (only glucose). x – means possible a little. xx – means medium. 0 – none detected.

CONCLUSION: B and C samples had some reducing sugar in them because they gave a positive test. After the practical we were told that B was starch powder and that C was dried milk so I am not sure where the sugar came fron in B unless some starch was changed by the boiling. A and D did not contain reducing sugar, not surprising as one was salt and the other baking powder. I tested a bit of bread off one of my sandwiches and it had about as much reducing sugar as the dried milk, but shot out of the tube when it boiled.

EXAMINER COMMENTS

Good standard. The student seems to be an able, practical scientist. The spoken instructions were obviously received, as the intent and method are restated well. Observations are good as far as they go, but a little more detail was possible. The only major problem for the student was **over enthusiasm** which led to a potentially hazardous situation with boiling bread. **This kind of ‘private’ science cannot be tolerated**. In fact, the next lesson involved further food tests and ‘real’ foods, so bread was tested safely and more thoroughly a few days later. If you have a bright idea, sound it out with your teacher first!

FURTHER SUGGESTIONS

This experiment: leads on to other food tests for starch, non-reducing sugars (e.g. sucrose), lipids, proteins, vitamin C, etc. and investigations with ‘real’ foods that are part of our diet.

Related practical work: investigating digestion and the effect of enzymes on food. Energy in foods (Chapter 4, Unit 3). Respiration and glucose.

UNIT 10 VARIATION, INHERITANCE AND EVOLUTION

10.1 Winkle variation

▸ **Syllabus link**

This is very much a biological topic area in science, but many other branches of science are pushing forward our understanding of the processes of **change**. According to the theory of **evolution**, living things change gradually from one generation to the next. Many people now accept that over millions of generations one species can change to produce a large number of new species.

It is thought that the process of evolution began on Earth some 4,000 million years ago. The science of inheritance, known as **genetics**, has explained how the characteristics of organisms are passed on to their offspring. Darwin's early work on evolution gave us a basic understanding of how slight **variations** between organisms can lead to new species being formed as the environment changes. The phrase ‘survival of the fittest’ sums up his theory reasonably well.

The coursework in this unit investigates the variation within a species, the edible winkle (Littorina littorea). This is the most widespread and is the commonest of the periwinkles, and it seems to have developed means for survival on almost all types of shore, its range even extending into estuaries. The exercise was designed to allow students to investigate variation practically and explore the ideas of **continuous** and **discontinuous variation** (see Revise Guide; Science pp. 112-113). It is variation within species that provides the opportunity for **natural selection** and evolutionary change.

Cross-references
Revise Guide; GCSE Science pp 105–19.

Coursework task
The students carried out the task during fieldwork at the seashore. After being shown what organisms they were to investigate by the teacher, they were asked to sample the populations in two different areas. One area was a very sheltered beach; the other was a slightly less sheltered harbour situation. Measurements of height or width were to be made for each animal in each sample. It was suggested that quadrats be used to randomly sample within each area, and that at least 100 animals should be measured at each sampling site. The data collected was to be processed and a size/frequency graph plotted.
A number of questions were asked:

1 What can you say about the patterns of distribution of sizes in the two locations?
2 What differences or similarities were there in the two samples?
3 What further investigations could be carried out to explain any patterns, differences or similarities you observed in your data from the two sites?

Copies of the questions were handed out to each student. The work was to be carried out in pairs, but reports were to be individually produced. Computer resources were made available to the students during the next few lessons, and at lunchtimes, so that they could use a 'statistics software package' to process their data.

Possible skills assessed in this coursework
Following instructions – Written (Chapter 2, Unit 2.2); Diagrams (Chapter 2, Unit 2.3); Selection and handling of apparatus (Chapter 2, Unit 3); Observing and measuring (Chapter 2, Unit 4); Recording and communication (Chapter 2, Unit 5). Interpreting information – Recognising patterns (Chapter 2, Unit 6.3); Drawing conclusions (Chapter 2, Unit 6.4); Identifying the problem and planning the investigation (Chapter 3, Unit 2).

Typical student's coursework

“ **The listed equipment details are adequate, but how did the student identify the L.*littorea* specimens? Was a key used? A known specimen provided for comparison?** ”

“ **What does the student mean by randomly? Why randomly? This is not explained, but obviously linked to obtaining a representative sample to measure. Not all the big ones!** ”

“ **Conservation of the shore observed - well done!** ”

“ **Diagram showing measurement taken is sensible and worthy of credit. Could have been more detailed with labels to show what kind of an animal was being investigatged.** ”

“ **Good. The aim is well stated and was obviously understood.** ”

Name –

FIELDWORK – GCSE Seashore visit

WINKLE STUDY

AIM
To investigate edible winkle populations in two areas of seashore by measuring individuals and drawing up size frequency bar charts so that the following questions might be answered:
What can you say about the patterns/types of distribution of sizes in the locations?
What differences or similarities were there in the two samples?
What further investigations could be carried out to explain any patterns, differences or similarities you observed in your data from the two sites?

EQUIPMENT
0.25m^2 plastic covered metal quadrat.
Waterproofed mm square graph paper.
Clipboard, paper & pencil.
} On seashore

BBC computer and ECOSOFT programs to process the data – back at college.

METHOD
A quadrat was randomly placed within the area to be investigated and all the winkles to be found in the 0.25m^2 were collected. Each specimen was measured and then returned to the area within the quadrat. Length was the measurement that was taken, as shown in the diagram below (Fig. 1).

Fig 1

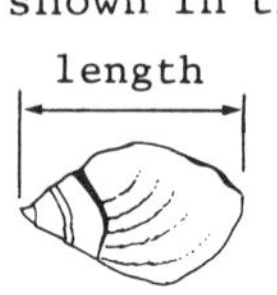

If there were less than 100 animals, then measurements were continued in an adjacent quadrat. The tables containing measurements were transferred to this report on return to college and a computer used to produce the

“What did the raw data look like? A tally score, or was a frequency table drawn up on site so patterns began to appear?”

“Results well presented, double columns a bit confusing, but does save space.”

“Size classes not clearly identified until the reader looks closely, but explanation is given.”

“The key ideas of CONTINUOUS and DISCONTINUOUS VARIATION have to be addressed, but not developed in the answer to Question 1. Perhaps the ideas of ‘normal distribution’ and ‘district groups’ should have been mentioned.”

“Question 2 is answered in a muddled way, good points are made but not clearly. Lists of similarities and differences as a starter at least!”

“Symbols for size classes and actual size classes still causing confusion. A pattern of use needs to be established and stuck to.”

“Some excellent ideas for further study, though it was intended that links should be made to the idea of natural selection operating differently in the two habitats. The beach was very sheltered, the harbour site was exposed to the open sea.”

size frequency bar charts for the two locations.

RESULTS

The raw measurements were transferred to this size frequency table:

SIZE CLASS (mm)	BEACH No. in class	HARBOUR No. in class	SIZE CLASS (mm)	BEACH No. in class	HARBOUR No. in class
* >1	0	0	>11	10	9
>2	0	2	>12	11	9
>3	3	2	>13	10	8
>4	3	0	>14	1	6
>5	2	4	>15	1	6
>6	12	5	>16	4	2
>7	14	12	>17	1	0
>8	11	13	>18	3	0
>9	16	16	>19	4	0
>10	10	11	>20	2	0

* >1 means greater than 1mm, but less than next size class which is >2 mm and so on.

ANSWERS TO QUESTIONS

1. In the harbour sample the pattern of distribution of size for the winkles seemed to fit the pattern I would expect for continuous variation, with more large winkles than small ones. In the beach sample variation looks rather more like discontinuous, with few small winkles and few large winkles, but nothing much in between. The greater than 3mm and greater than 13 mm being the limits of the large number groups.

2. Groups I and G were very well represented in both samples, but the beach sample had the greatest numbers outside the really abundant middle range. The I size class was most common in both samples. In the beach sample a wider range was abundant.

3. Further investigations might be to:

(i) See if size is related to age.
(ii) To check that all the sizes are of the same species. In the beach sample the really big ones could be another type.
(iii) What happens to the big ones from the harbour?
(iv) How are conditions different in the two places?
(v) If the size is equal to age, maybe fewer are born some years?
(vi) What feeds on winkles? People?

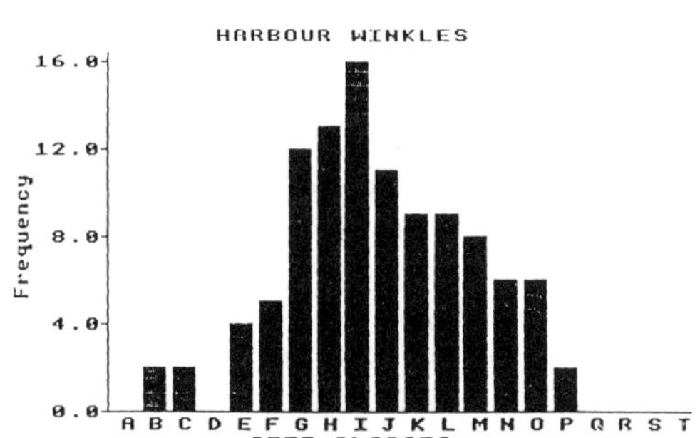

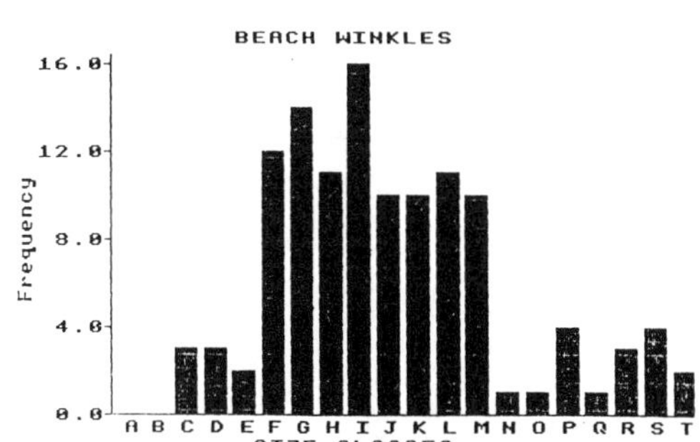

“Computer generated graphics are excellent, and indicate sensible use of I.T. (information technology).”

“Key to size classes could be improved, obviously a short cut!”

*KEY TO SIZE CLASSES

A:	>1	B:	>2
C:	>3	D:	>4
E:	>5	F:	>6
G:	>7	H:	>8
I:	>9	J:	>10
K:	>11	L:	>12
M:	>13	N:	>14
O:	>15	P:	>16
Q:	>17	R:	>18
S:	>19	T:	>20

EXAMINER COMMENTS

A **good** standard of work, thorough but still lacking the polish that the best pieces of work had. The collection of data in the field was done efficiently and the analysis using the computer was impressive. The task of interpretation was a difficult one and some rough planning of the answers to the first two questions would have raised the quality of the final product significantly.

FURTHER SUGGESTIONS

This experiment: the answers to the third question would take this task further, and student-organised research could easily form a follow-up fieldwork exercise involving a whole range of other skills.

Related experiments: there are close links between variation and genetics, right through to work on the mechanism of evolution. Tongue rolling, present or absent ear lobes, left and right curled cuckoo-pint flowers and many other examples of single-gene inheritance could be investigated as examples of discontinuous variation. Measuring differences in humans provides interesting information on continuous variation if index finger length, height or weight are measured.

UNIT 11 ECOLOGY

11.1 Quadrats – plant populations

- **Syllabus link**

Ecology is the study of the relationships between the living and non-living factors in the environment. Because the topic involves the 'world' outside the laboratory, practical work is a must. You may get involved in a 'field trip' or simply spend a few lessons in the school or college grounds. A practical starting point for many students will involve sampling plants. As plants do not move, sampling an area for them is not too difficult. The most basic piece of equipment is called a *quadrat*, and is usually square. The quadrat used in the coursework below was made of plastic-covered wire and measured 0.5m × 0.5m.

This device can be used in a variety of ways. Plants can be recorded as in it, or not, at the simplest level (which is what the student below chose to do). Though, perhaps the most useful way to use it is to *estimate* how much of the area each plant type covers inside the quadrat, and write this down as a 'percentage cover'. Often it is impossible to actually count the number of plants of each type even though it seems the most logical thing to do. Usually, lots of quadrat readings are taken to give a representative sample of an area. Where to put the quadrat is a problem you should not choose! Once you have identified the area of study, samples should be taken randomly. **Don't throw the quadrat** – you will lose marks and get into trouble! Throw something soft, like a plastic bag with a bit of sand in it, but first close your eyes, get a friend to turn you round, then throw the bag over your shoulder. Now place your quadrat where it lands. A better way is to use pairs of random numbers to find those random spots, a bit like treasure-seeking, as the student in this example did.

- **Cross-references**

Revise Guide; GCSE Science, pp 120-36.

- **Coursework task**

The teacher talked to the students about plant distribution and sampling while out in the school grounds. They tried out different ways of sampling with a quadrat and discussed them as a class. They then returned to the laboratory and planned an investigation of their own, in groups of three. They were told to base their work on a question that they might answer by gathering scientific evidence using the quadrating technique. Each student was to write up an individual report and was given that lesson plus following homework to complete it.

Use of a quadrat

- **Possible skills assessed in this coursework**

Following instructions – Spoken (Chapter 2, Unit 2.1); Selection and handling of apparatus (Chapter 2, Unit 3); Observing and measuring (Chapter 2, Unit 4); Recording and communication (Chapter 2, Unit 5).

Interpreting information – Recognising patterns (Chapter 2, Unit 6.3); Drawing conclusions (Chapter 2, Unit 6.4); Identifying the problem and planning the investigation (Chapter 3, Unit 2); Evaluating the experiment and suggesting improvements (Chapter 3, Unit 5); Designing an experiment and an appropriate control (Chapter 3, Unit 4).

▶ Typical student's coursework

"Hypothesis could have been more concisely stated."

"Good point. Chose plants that they could identify, rather than all plants. More likely to get the job done!"

"Control samples taken in non-pitch areas, good scientific method."

"Control of other variables?"

"Seem well organised as a group, sharing out the jobs to be done."

"Chose to use the random numbers technique, rather than have the 'fun' of throwing things about. Well done!"

"Diagram of quadrat probably a waste of time, written in method anyway."

"Results table excellent though raw data (ticks) have disappeared. This is obviously processed data."

"Kind of plant? Type would be a more technical word."

"Double bar chart an excellent idea, no doubt lifted from a text. Very well done!"

FIELDWORK: plant populations "**Sensible, though not original question.**"

QUESTION: Does the trampling caused by players affect the plants on the games pitches?

HYPOTHESIS: When we went outside and looked at the pitches and other areas of the school fields it seemed there was a difference, so plant populations do get affected by the playing of sports.

METHOD: We chose 9 common plants that we could easily identify more or less exactly and also added bare earth to the list as it seemed important. To sample the pitches and other areas of the fields we used a quadrat that was 0.5m × 0.5m square. One of the group drew up a chart on which to record the results and collected a clipboard to use on the field. We picked our games area and put the quadrat down 25 times randomly inside it using the random numbers we had been given to mark the random spots. At each spot we ticked whether each of the 10 things was in the square, so we counted how frequently each turned up in 25 squares. Next we did the same for an area where no games are played.

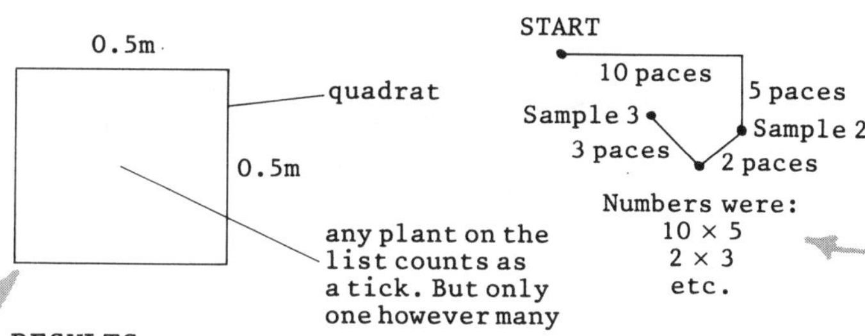

"**Diagram explaining it useful, but small and confusing.**"

RESULTS

No.	Kind of plant	School fields: NOT PITCHES	School fields: PITCHES
1	Daisy	21	8
2	Dandelion	17	0
3	Clover	14	6
4	Plantain	12	3
5	Buttercup	7	2
6	Dock	4	2
7	Yarrow	13	3
8	Speedwell	20	8
9	Grass	25	25
10	Bare ground	1	23

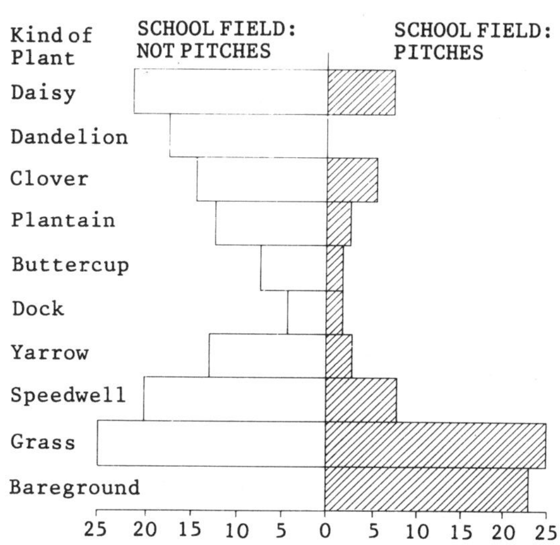

"**Unlabelled axis – 'frequency of plant type in 25 samples' or similar.**"

CONCLUSIONS: The bar chart shows that there is a big difference in the

Good. To the point and refers to the original hypothesis, but no reference to control.

Sensible evaluation, so why did they choose the tick/frequency technique?

Some excellent points made and/or remembered! Identification? Size? Being investigated?

populations of the different types of plants so our hypothesis was correct, trampling does affect the plants.

CRITICISMS: We could easily have done more than 25 samples in each place which would have made our results much better. Some of the plants might have been identified wrongly, there were several sorts of some of the plants such as clover and dandelion. Just ticking if plants are present is not a good method because grass was in all the squares, but not as much in the pitch samples. Also some plants are big and important, others are very tiny. Area covered by the plants would give better results so next we should do % covered in each quadrat.

Quadrat on untrampled field

EXAMINER COMMENTS

High standard. The student has obviously had the time to complete the task and perhaps it is a bit 'wordy', considering what it achieves. However, there are many new questions hinted at by those fascinating results. What a pity that the student found no opportunity to discuss them within the report.

FURTHER SUGGESTIONS

This experiment: why are some plant types plentiful in both areas? Why are some plentiful only in one area? What does trampling do to the soil? How do a plant's adaptations help?

Related practical work: soil testing for water, air, compaction, nutrients etc. Colonisation/reproduction (sexual and vegetative) studies.

Linked work: Chapter 4, Unit 10.

UNIT 12 THE SOLAR SYSTEM, WEATHER AND ROCKS

12.1 Mineral hardness testing

Syllabus link

The mineral wealth of a country is one very important factor which can affect its economic growth. In the past, deposits of coal and iron ore, and more recently, deposits of oil have increased the strength of the British economy. In investigations of rocks and minerals there is much work in classification, identification and grouping. This has relevance to chemistry through processes such as metal extraction and a knowledge of the sources of chemicals in common use.

Physical characteristics, such as density and hardness, can easily be investigated in the laboratory, and form the basis of the coursework described in this Unit. To geologists, coal and oil are not thought of as minerals; they are too variable in their composition and have far from constant physical properties. Minerals, in the geological sense of the word, do vary slightly in their properties, but the variation is strictly limited by the internal arrangements of their atoms. This almost constant composition for a given mineral can usually be expressed by means of a chemical formula, which may be very simple (e.g. iron pyrites or 'fool's gold' – FeS_2) or very complex (e.g. garnet – Ca, Mg, Fe, Mn, Al silicate) if many elements are present.

Hardness, or resistance to scratching, was a very early development in the identification of minerals. An Austrian mineralogist called Mohs devised a scale of increasing hardness with 'talc' at level 1 and diamond at level 10. The scale is still in common use today. Rough guides to hardness can be used in the field, with finger nail at about 2.5 and penknife at about 5.5 on Mohs' scale.

Cross-references

Revise Guide; GCSE Science pp 138–54, 161–4, 234–9.

Coursework task

The coursework task presented by the teacher was seemingly a simple one. The instructions were spoken. The students were told that hard minerals will scratch softer minerals, and that they were to devise a test to put four given minerals into order, from the hardest to the softest. Students were asked to pay attention to the design of their experiments, record their observations and present their results in a suitable form. Lastly, they were to draw together their findings into a conclusion that placed each mineral on a scale 1-4.

Possible skills assessed in this coursework

Following instructions – spoken (Chapter 2, Unit 2.1); Observing and measuring (Chapter 2, Unit 4); Recording and communication (Chapter 2, Unit 5).
Interpreting information – Recognising patterns (Chapter 2, Unit 6.3); Drawing conclusions (Chapter 2, Unit 6.4); Identifying the problem and planning the investigation (Chapter 3, Unit 2).

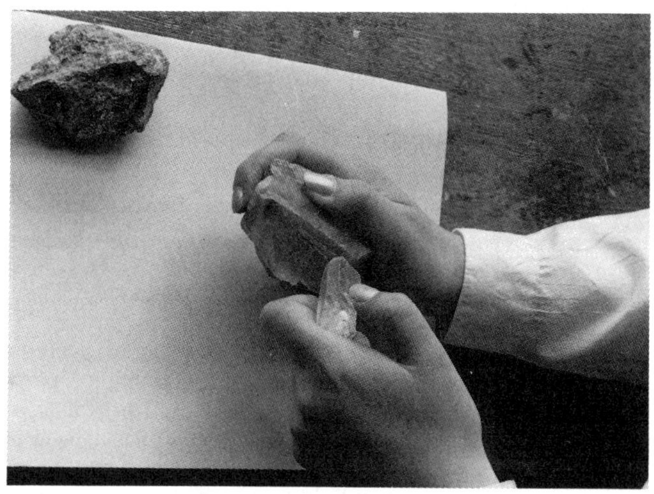

Typical student's coursework

HARDNESS TESTS
We had to see which was the strongest. We scraped one rock on another and wrote down what happened in the results.

RESULTS

	FLUORITE	GYPSUM	CALCITE	QUARTZ
QUARTZ	scratched	broke into bits	nothing	X
CALCITE	nothing	scratch	X	nothing
GYPSUM	crumbled	X	nothing	split up
FLUORITE	X	scratch	Fell in two	nothing

CONCLUSION The quartz was the best because nothing else did anything to it. Then the calcite and gypsum and the fluorite was last.

"Has the student a clear idea of what is being investigated?"

"Good. Idea of table is correct."

"Idea of not testing two of the same minerals is correct."

"Far from clear record of what happened – which rock scratched which?"

"Was a clean fresh surface used each time?"

"Poor. Records not consistent; different kinds of observations have been used."

"Clearly the student is confusing the ideas of hardness, strength and fracture. It seems that the materials have probably been treated more roughly than was intended or necessary."

"The interpretation of results shows the failure of the recording methods. The student has not a clear understanding of the task."

EXAMINER COMMENTS

Low standard. This is a below-average attempt at this sort of exercise. The student failed to identify the problem that was given. The idea of presenting a table was a good one, but the observations failed to provide a basis for sensible conclusions to be made. The student used too many variables, scratching (as was instructed), crumbling, splitting up, falling in two etc. There had already been some mention of Mohs' scale (1-talc, 2-gypsum, 3-calcite, 4-fluorspar, 5-apatite, 6-orthoclase, 7-quartz, 8-topaz, 9-corundum and 10-diamond) in which minerals can scratch ones lower down the scale and can be scratched by those above. The student seems to have missed this information, or not understood it.

FURTHER SUGGESTIONS

This experiment: leads into other forms of rock and mineral testing such as 'streak' and 'cleavage'.

Related experiments: flame testing, acid testing for carbonates and metal extraction from minerals/ores.

UNIT 13 MATTER AND PARTICLES

13.1 Diffusion of gases

- **Syllabus link**

This unit is linked to the idea that all matter is made from atoms, molecules and particles. **Molecules** are the smallest single pieces of a material. You could 'chop up' a molecule such as water, but it would become **atoms** of hydrogen and oxygen gas. Atoms are the smallest units of an **element**. In any one element there will be only one sort of atom, and these cannot be broken down chemically into anything simpler.

Particles may be made up of a number of molecules. Investigations in this part of science often involves looking at particles, such as pollen grains (as did Robert Brown in the 1800's when he discovered what we now know as **Brownian Motion**, smoke in air or toothpaste in water.

Often this whole area of science is found under the heading **kinetic theory**. It sounds grand, but is only the view that all matter (solid, liquid or gas) is made up of particles which are in constant motion. This piece of coursework concerns the observation and explanation of **diffusion**, just one of a series of phenomena which can be understood when you apply kinetic theory.

- **Cross-references**

Revise Guide; GCSE Science, pp 153–173.

- **Coursework task**

The students had seen this experiment in a text and after discussion with their teacher it was agreed that they set it up as a practical exercise. The task was to compare the rates of diffusion of two different gases. This was to be done in a sealed system as in the text book (see Revise Guide; Science pp 156), but they were also to devise a means for the detection of the 'progress' of the gases inside the system. The instructions were given during the discussion (although their text provided outline guidance also!) and students were asked to work in groups of three maximum, each writing up an individual report.

The teacher suggested that the skills of observation, recording, and making conclusions would receive close attention for assessment purposes.

- **Possible skills assessed in this coursework**

Following instructions – Written (Chapter 2, Unit 2.2); Diagrams (Chapter 2, Unit 2.3); Selection and handling of apparatus (Chapter 2, Unit 3); Observing and measuring (Chapter 2, Unit 4); Recording and communication (Chapter 2, Unit 5). Interpreting information – Recognising patterns (Chapter 2, Unit 6.3); Drawing conclusions (Chapter 2, Unit 6.4); Identifying the problem and planning the investigation (Chapter 3, Unit 2); Following safe working procedures (Chapter 2, Unit 7); Working with others (Chapter 2, Unit 8); Evaluating the experiment and suggesting improvements (Chapter 3, Unit 5).

Typical student's coursework

DIFFUSION SPEEDS – practical

AIM. To compare the diffusion speeds of two gases (HCl and NH_3)

APPARATUS

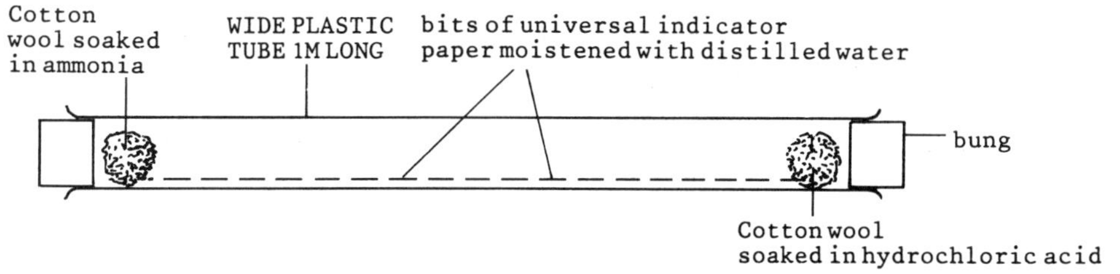

METHOD. We put some ammonia (very strong!) in some cotton wool and put it in the plastic tube held in two retort stands. We put a rubber bung over the end. We did the same at the other end at the same time but we used hydrochloric acid (strong!). First we had put bits of universal indicator paper which we had put one drop of water (distilled) on spaced out along the bottom of the tube to detect the acid or ammonia gases. These were sort of orange, but some were green. Then we left the apparatus for 20 minutes and watched what happened.

RESULTS. Some of the bits of indicator paper went red at the acid end and some went blue at the other end. About half way between there was a circle of white substance and a sort of white smoke.

CONCLUSION. The particles of the acid and ammonia have been moved along the tube. The particles of air are constantly moving in all directions. They have bumped into the acid and ammonia and knocked them along the tube. The universal indicator went red by the acid and blue by the ammonia so it must be alkali.

“Kinetic theory more or less understood.”

CRITICISMS. We should have measured the time from the start when the bits of paper changed colour to see which gas went fastest, and also where the ring was in tube which would have told us the same fact. We did not really achieve what we were supposed to do and should of thought more before starting.

“Failed to comprehend movement of the molecules of the chemicals themselves.”

“Realistic criticisms, and a hard hitting last comment! Think first, then do!”

“Good. Aim clearly stated.”

“Generally good diagram, though rather small.”

“The acid and alkali were concentrated and precautions should have been taken.”

“Keen but verbose! What is wrong with – ‘the apparatus was set up as shown in the diagram’?”

“Thoughts not put in order before writing, and they do matter in this experiment!”

“Some confusion over the universal indicator papers showing neutrality.”

“Good observations and clear detail of the appearance of the region where the gases met.”

“Results record is poor.”

“No timing or comment on speed, yet they did observe?”

“No mention of relative distance – how many pieces of paper were blue, how many red? Where did the gases meet?”

“Has not used information provided by colour changes in the pieces of universal indicator paper on the relative speed of movement.”

EXAMINER COMMENTS

Clearly a keen student, but not necessarily a good ‘practising scientist’ yet. **Moderate** to **good** standard. At least the student seemed to know where there was a weakness. Having the aim in mind is important, and was the biggest single failing in this coursework example. The student obviously realised too late what should have been done!

FURTHER SUGGESTIONS

This experiment: some effort to make it quantitative by measuring time, perhaps using a longer tube would reveal something about the link between size of particle and speed of diffusion.

Related practical work: investigating diffusion in liquids and gels ($KMnO_4$) in water and agar). Other kinetic theory experiments and models abound, expansion and contraction, osmosis, changes of state etc.

Linked work: exchange of gases in respiration (see Revise Guide; Science, pp 94–5), absorption of food into the blood from the gut (Revise Guide; Science, pp 91–2), exchanges between blood and cells of the body (Revise Guide; Science, p 91), etc.

ACKNOWLEDGEMENTS

I am most grateful to Di Barton, who as Title Adviser assisted greatly in adding the finishing touches to the manuscript, and indeed, for her contributions throughout the book.

My thanks also go to the Science Staff at Ivybridge Community College for their help and advice, in particular Malcolm Carter, Bob Cawthorne and Perry Price for their writing and selection of coursework, John Ogg for his considerable contribution to Chapter 2 and, of course, the students whose work appears anonymously.

I also acknowledge my gratitude for J.M. Inghams's excellent coursework activities, which originated at St Ivo School in Cambridgeshire.

All the photographs that add much to this book were taken by Andrew Willson, a sixth-form science student at Ivybridge Community College. I hope this is the first of many successes for him.

I am very grateful to Geoff Black and Stuart Wall for their encouragement, guidance and patience in editing this book.

I acknowledge with gratitude permission to print extracts from syllabuses and other documents from the following: HMSO for the various National Criteria; London and East Anglian Group; Midland Examining Group; Northern Examining Association; Northern Ireland Schools Examinations Council; Southern Examining Group; Welsh Joint Education Committee; International GCSE.

I take complete responsibility for my interpretation of the syllabuses of the Examining Groups.

Finally I thank my wife, Nicola, and family for their understanding and support during the writing of this book.